HOW TO RAISE A GLOBAL CITIZEN

HOW TO RAISE A GLOBAL CITIZEN

FOR THE PARENTS OF THE CHILDREN WHO WILL SAVE THE WORLD

ANNA DAVIDSON

Author and Editor Anna Davidson
Designer Mandy Earey
Senior Editor Alastair Laing
US Editor Jennette ElNaggar
Jacket Designer Amy Cox
Jackets Coordinator Lucy Philpott
Production Editor Heather Blagden
Senior Production Controller Luca Bazzoli
Managing Editor Dawn Henderson
Managing Art Editor Marianne Markham
Art Director Maxine Pedliham
Publishing Director Katie Cowan

Illustrated by Cecilia Castelli

First American Edition, 2021
Published in the United States by DK Publishing
1450 Broadway, Suite 801, New York, NY 10018

The authorized representative in the EEA is
Dorling Kindersley Verlag GmbH. Arnulfstr. 124,
80636 Munich, Germany

For text copyright details, see p.224
Copyright © 2021 Dorling Kindersley Limited
DK, a Division of Penguin Random House LLC
21 22 23 24 25 10 9 8 7 6 5 4 3 2 1
001–324818–Sep/2021

A catalog record for this book is available from the Library of Congress.
ISBN 978-0-7440-4208-5

Printed and bound in China.

For the curious
www.dk.com

MIX
Paper from
responsible sources
FSC™ C018179

This book was made with Forest Stewardship Council ™ certified
paper – one small step in DK's commitment to a sustainable future.
For more information go to www.dk.com/our-green-pledge

CONTENTS

● PLAY TOGETHER 159

● EXPLORE TOGETHER 187

INTRODUCTION

What is it like to grow up in the 2020s? I can't answer that question with any certainty—and I imagine that, if asked, every child would give a different response. I suspect that it feels very different from growing up in the 20th century, as the majority of parents of today's school-aged children did. For all that the 1980s and '90s are the recent past, so much has changed.

The idea of being a "global citizen" is at the heart of what is different now. We are so connected. Globalization means we buy food, clothing, toys, and tech that have been grown, sewn, manufactured, and developed all over the world. Social media and streaming services mean we think no more of messaging a friend in another country with a quip about a shared viewing experience than we do of messaging a friend down the road. Boundaries of geography and nationality are blurred. Yet our identity is as important as ever, and being a citizen of the whole globe is an important aspect of who we are, whether we realize it or not.

Parents everywhere want to raise their children to be happy, healthy, and able to thrive in the world as it exists today. This means instilling values, such as empathy, compassion, respect, and open-mindedness, that will allow them to make deep and inclusive friendships, online as well as in person. It means giving them age-appropriate knowledge and understanding of different cultures and countries and an awareness of other people's stories and identities. It means encouraging them to make constructive connections that build communities up instead of tearing them apart, from the family unit to our global society.

Parents also want to prepare their children for a future we can't imagine. We know there is a climate crisis and that it is the new generation who stand to lose the most. We owe it to them to teach them to think critically and creatively about how the world works and give them the tools, confidence, and knowledge to invent, speak out, and take action to make it a better place—one in which they can grow old.

This book explores what it means to be a global citizen in a very practical way. Each chapter covers a different aspect of parenting a 21st-century child, and each contributor brings their own unique perspective. Between us, we are parents to 16 children from the ages of 3 to 15. I hope you will find the blogs in each chapter thought-provoking and inspiring. For instant practical tips and ideas, turn to the Action Plans at the end of each section.

The future is bright. It is because of our children. Children have the energy, capacity, and passion to be aware of and understand their place in the wider world; to take an active role in their community; and to work with others to make our planet more peaceful, sustainable, and fairer for all. Every child deserves a happy childhood. Parents and carers can help their own children find and share the joy that the world has to offer and, in doing so, experience the inner pleasure and fulfillment that this brings.

Anna Davidson

Anna Davidson

MEET THE
BLOGGERS

Find out all about the seven international contributors whose blogs you'll discover in the pages of this book. Each writer reveals their passions and motivations.

MARVYN HARRISON

Marvyn Harrison is a father of two and founder of Dope Black CIC as well as cofounder of the Diversity, Equity, and Inclusion (DEI) consultancy BELOVD. He coined the term "Dope Black Dads" on Father's Day 2018. Challenged by his feelings toward parenthood, Marvyn created a WhatsApp group with fathers he knew, hoping to share and learn from the experiences of those going on a similar journey to him. Now the Dope Black Dads network engages more than 12,000 dads across the UK, US, and Africa. Marvyn regularly leads podcasts for parents and contributes to panels, webinars, Q&As, and documentaries on the subjects of male parenting, masculinity, mental health, the Black experience, and business.

dopeblack.org
@DopeBlackDads

DR ANNABELLE HUMANES

Dr. Annabelle Humanes wants o live in a world where diversity is celebrated and valued. A linguist, she worked in academia for more than a decade before starting a family, teaching languages, and carrying out research in language acquisition in young children. Evidence-based decision-making and multilingualism are her passions, and her own family lives with four languages (and cultures) on a daily basis. When she is not traveling or eating her way around the world with her little European citizens, she runs language enrichment classes and playgroups for French-speaking families. She blogs about being the mother of two cross-cultural children and blending cultures and languages.

thepiripirilexicon.com
Insta: @ThePiriPiriLexicon

DR MELERNIE MEHEUX

JAMES MURRAY

Dr. Melernie Meheux is a senior educational psychologist passionate about using psychology to support children and their families. As a certified play therapist, she believes in the power of play to give children a voice to make sense of their experiences and strongly advocates the rights of all children to play. Melernie is cochair of the British Psychological Society's Division of Educational and Child Psychology (DECP) and chair of the board of trustees for Solidarity Sports, a charity that supports disadvantaged children and those who have experienced trauma to access play opportunities. She loves writing, hates inequality, and wants to contribute toward saving the planet in any way that she can!

bps.org.uk/blogs
@DrMelsie

James Murray is an environmental journalist and founding editor of the award-winning website BusinessGreen. He has spent the past 15 years reporting on the climate crisis, the green economy, and clean technologies and is a regular commentator on a wide range of environmental issues on TV and radio. In 2020, he also helped launch the world's first Net Zero Festival, bringing together business leaders, policymakers, and campaigners to explore how to accelerate the green industrial revolution. An English graduate from the University of Exeter, James lives in South London with his wife and two sons.

businessgreen.com
@James_BG

JEN PANARO

Jen Panaro is a self-proclaimed composting nerd and an advocate for eco-friendly living for modern families. As a mom to two boys, she is passionate about helping families find ways to be more responsible stewards to our communities and the planet. She regularly writes for her blog, Honestly Modern, and other publications about exploring climate action, zero-waste living, regenerative gardening, and intersectional environmentalism, all through the lens of modern family life. Jen is also the founder of WasteWell, a company she runs that provides composting services and related educational resources. In her spare time, she's a messy gardener and a serial library book borrower.

honestlymodern.com
Insta: @HonestlyModern

"Being a global citizen is a way of living. We are connected by our passions and our values as we raise the next generation, not divided by our different nationalities and varying interpretations of history. We all have a perspective to offer and a future to share."

JESS PURCELL

Jess Purcell is a science educator who is dedicated to making the science of sustainability accessible to all learners. She creates sustainability science experiments and nature activities for students of all ages, which can be done in the classroom or at home and are designed to foster critical thinking skills and a love of the natural world. Jess lives in central Pennsylvania with her husband, two kids, and two cats and can usually be found outside, working out the kinks of an experiment, upcycling trash into "treasure," hiking with her family, or attempting to read a book while being cajoled into a game of hide and seek.

thoughtfullysustainable.com
Insta: @ThoughtfullySustainable

FARIBA SOETAN

Fariba Soetan is a blogger and mother of three multiracial daughters living in London. Her passion for raising citizens of the world grew from her own experience being raised in a mixed heritage family (Iranian/British) and immigrating from Tehran, Iran, to Edmonton, Canada, at a very young age. After meeting her Nigerian husband in Wales, Fariba moved to Nigeria for a few years with her two young children before settling down in London. Her blog for parents of mixed race children, Mixed.up.Mama, aims to help bridge parents' understanding about raising multiracial families and encourage them to be intentional about talking about race and identity to children.

mixedracefamily.com
Insta: @Mixed.Up.Mama

LOVE THE PLANET

All over the globe, our fellow citizens are struggling with the impact of climate change. Empower your child to understand and care for our extraordinary planet.

UNDERSTAND OUR WORLD

If we care for our children's future, we must care for their planet—and that means teaching them why they should care, too.

Our planet is amazing. It provides us with food to eat, shelter to keep us warm and dry, and the natural resources for ingenious humans to create wonderful luxuries and necessities for survival. However, it can be hard for a child whose food appears in front of them ready-prepared and whose clothes are bought finished from a store to make the connection to the Earth—let alone realize how dependent on it we are for survival. Right now, all around the world, our fellow citizens are struggling with the effects of climate change brought about by human actions.

WARMING UP

Planet Earth is now more than 1.8 degrees Fahrenheit hotter than it wasin preindustrial times, and scientists predict that, at current rates of increase, by the time today's 10-year-old is 90, it will be another 2 to 3 degrees warmer. The effects of even this 1.8-degree change can already be seen: a higher frequency of more extreme forest fires and storms, sea levels that worldwide have risen by about 7 in (18 cm) since 1900, the collapse of ecosystems such as coral reefs, and the extinction of species.

The temperature change is caused mainly by our burning of fossil fuels to provide energy to power our homes, our businesses, our transportation. Burning coal, gas, and oil sends carbon dioxide into the atmosphere, which acts like a blanket over the planet, soaking up the heat radiation from the Earth's surface. Trees usefully absorb carbon dioxide, but many trees have been cut down, as mass deforestation has cleared the ground for lucrative crops, such as soy and palm oil.

DIVERSITY AT RISK

The natural world is a complex intermeshing of mutually dependent living things, including humans. Biodiversity simply means Earth's wide variety of plant and animal species, living in their natural environment, interacting with each other and with the physical world. Biodiversity gives us a world full of wonders. What's more, we require it to survive. The clean air that we breathe, the plants and animals that we need for food—these all rely on biodiversity.

Climate change and deforestation have a negative impact on biodiversity, and so, too, do human actions such as destroying natural habitats by converting them into farms, factories, and cities. Activities such as overfishing reduce stocks to critical levels, and mining and drilling use

resources faster than they are created. Around 1 million plant and animal species are threatened with extinction, and we have already lost the first mammal due to climate change— the Bramble Cay melomys, a tiny rodent native to a low-lying island in Queensland, Australia. Ultimately, loss of biodiversity means a world without the resources we depend on.

BIGGER THAN US

Climate change and biodiversity are complicated subjects to explain, but children instinctively appreciate that they are part of something bigger than themselves. Even a newborn baby knows how it feels to be too hot, and children are often far more in touch with nature than adults are, as they race around, crunch fall leaves underfoot, splash in a puddle, roll in the snow. A teenager can feel a deep connection with a family pet, and a toddler can be absorbed watching creepy-crawlies. A 100-year-old tree in the park can feel calming to all ages.

Everything we have, from a plastic toy to water to drink, has been provided by the planet. By helping your child connect the dots so they understand our place within Earth's ecosystems, you may find that they become the ones urging you to save fellow citizens by saving the planet.

JEN PANARO

THE UNIVERSE IN BOOKS

Every night before my boys go to sleep, we sit down on the floor next to one of their beds and read aloud together. We read a mix of fun chapter books, silly picture books, and deeper stories I select with intention.

Since they were young, I've made a concerted effort to bring books into our home that help my boys understand our small place in this big, amazing world. We read books about other cultures, the importance of kindness, and the value of the natural world, among so many other topics.

Thank goodness for our local library, or we might have spent a small fortune on all the books we've explored together. Week after week, we carry home heavy bags of picture books (maximum 99 per card) about the poignant beauty of Mother Nature, the importance of diversity in our ecosystems, and the impact that our actions have on the land and our lives locally and around the world.

Although some of these topics feel heavy, children's book authors and illustrators are amazingly skilled at presenting deep and complex issues in ways children can digest and appreciate. The content inspires questions that breed more robust discussions about climate change, the regeneration of the planet's resources, and our role in helping heal the Earth.

> *"Gorgeous illustrations draw in their imaginations and inspire our discussions about the natural world."*

I have shared a few of our very favorite books in the Resources section (see p.216). These books showcase the magical mystery of the natural world we can't always see, the beauty that flourishes when we care for even the simplest of flowers and weeds, and ingenious ways we can overcome the tumultuous effects of climate change in communities. May we all find a few books that help us know the world we cannot see from our own eyes.

JAMES MURRAY

GENERATION REVOLUTION

Every generation thinks it is born at a turning point in history, but for a child born today, it is true. They are fated to join what is one of the scariest and most exciting eras since the first Mesopotamian tribes learned to harvest crops.

Atmospheric concentrations of carbon dioxide have not been this high since the time when forests grew near the South Pole, 3 million years ago. Consequently, the 2010s were the hottest decade ever recorded. The last month to deliver temperatures below the 20th-century average was February 1985, and we are living through a wave of extinctions.

Children can expect to experience a century defined by an unprecedented pace of climatic change. Dying coral reefs, rising seas, and expanding deserts are the most evocative parts of this crisis. Hard-nosed analysts from military academies and global insurers now join environmental activists to warn

of worsening food security, inundated coastal cities, and escalating conflicts.

Some argue that faced with such threats it is wrong to bring children into the world. No one should be judged for their reproductive choices, of course, but a community that opts wholesale not to bring forward a new generation, that ceases to see children as a social good, is surely finished regardless of the planetary risks it faces.

"Children need to understand the world they are part of, both the good and the bad."

Because the flip side of this environmental insecurity is that we've entered an age of epic possibilities. Ours is the first generation since the earliest humans harnessed fire an estimated 400,000 years ago that has to figure out how to power their societies without burning stuff. We are experiencing the fastest, most dramatic, and potentially most life-affirming technological revolution in history. From wind turbines to electric vehicles, clean technologies hold the promise not just of salvation but of health and prosperity for all.

This tension between environmental optimism and pessimism has always reminded me of the initial sleep-deprived buzz of parenthood itself—that mix of unbridled joy combined with fear you may not be up to the task, that things could go terribly wrong.

How then to explain such high stakes without leaving a child scared or daunted? For me, the starting point is to heed the advice of Greta Thunberg and tell the truth. That truth should be presented with nuance and sympathy, but there is no point hiding it. Children need to understand the world they are part of, the good and the bad.

The basic principles of education apply to climate change as much as anything else. There's huge value in providing children with clear facts and concepts and letting them reach their own conclusions. I remember the lesson from my school days with stinging clarity. The diagram on the blackboard showed how a blanket of gases captured heat that bounced around the atmosphere,

gradually sending temperatures skyward. I recall thinking, "Something's broken, why isn't everyone working to fix it?" With the self-righteousness only a teenager can possess, I interpreted climate change as a challenge to overcome, not an enemy to cower before.

Our boys are too young to be interested in climate change, but when the time comes, we'll tell them the climate is changing and humans are causing it, that the changes under way are serious and dangerous. We'll also tell them every generation has its existential challenges and this is ours; that we have the technologies and policies to avert catastrophe and build a better world; that we can rewild and recover natural habitats, switch to clean energy, and build sustainable economies that benefit everyone.

Most important of all, we'll try to show how we all have a role to play in this mission. As one of my favorite climate writers, the US scientist Kate Marvel, argues, "we need courage, not hope" in the face of climate change. "Courage is the resolve to do well without the assurance of a happy ending," she writes. There are few more important lessons.

JESS PURCELL

GREENHOUSE EXPERIMENT

Here's a simple experiment I've done at home with my son and daughter to help them understand the links between our actions and their effects.

Think of a blanket of gases covering the Earth. This "blanket" holds in heat. Without it, Earth would be a freezing cold rock! The gases, known as greenhouse gases, include molecules such as water vapor, carbon dioxide, methane, and many others. The problem arises when the blanket gets thicker, trapping more heat than is necessary, thus increasing the average global temperature of the planet.

Each bottle represents the Earth's biosphere. The antacid tablet reacts with the water to produce carbon dioxide, just as burning fossil fuels does.

Equipment

2 two-liter clear plastic or glass bottles; 2 thermometers; 1 effervescent antacid tablet; clay; water; timer; heat source (incandescent light, hair dryer, or the summer sun!)

Procedure

1 Fill each bottle half full of water. Label one bottle "A" and the other "B."
2 Seal the tops of both bottles with clay.
3 Insert a thermometer through the clay for both bottles, being sure to leave no gaps for air to enter.
4 Measure and record the initial internal air temperature of each bottle.
5 If indoors, place the bottles in front of the heat source. If outdoors, place them in direct summer sunlight.
6 Remove the thermometer in bottle B and add the antacid tablet, broken into small pieces, to the water. Replace the thermometer.
7 Observe and record the temperature of each bottle every 5 minutes for 20 minutes.

Within 20 minutes, with the "sun" shining brightly, you should see a noticeable difference in temperature between the two bottles. The one with excess carbon dioxide will record a higher temperature.

My eight-year-old was amazed at how much hotter the bottle with excess carbon dioxide was, which led to a great discussion on how our daily actions can affect the climate. My five-year-old simply loved watching the tablet fizz!

CHERISH THE PLANET'S BOUNTY, SO THE WHOLE WORLD CAN SHARE IT.

ACTION PLAN
Discover Nature

In our screen-based lives, it's easy to lose sight of our connection to the natural world. Help your child discover more about their environment.

SIT SPOT

Establish a "sit spot" with your child—a place outside your front door or farther afield where you can both sit in silence together once a day or once a week to observe the natural world around you. If you can't get to a forest or a field, there is plenty of nature to spot in the city!

NATURE NOTES

Make a point of finding out more about the flora and fauna you see around you every day. You could keep a log or a photo diary of the plants you pass on your way to school each morning, noting how they change with the seasons. An app on your phone can help you identify exactly what plant or flower you are looking at.

PUDDLE PLAY

Puddles are magical for young children. Let your child jump and splash, in Wellington boots in the winter or barefoot in the summer. Try drawing a chalk outline around a puddle and observe how its size shrinks or grows throughout the day.

ADOPT AN ANIMAL

Does your older child have a favorite animal? Encourage them to research it online, using reputable websites such as the World Wide Fund for Nature (WWF) to find out its natural habitat and learn about any risks the species faces. They could even contribute some pocket money to an "adopt an animal" program to help protect an endangered species.

WORM WATCH

Take a magnifying glass and trowel to a flower bed and discover worms busying away in the soil. Be careful if you touch them since earthworms breathe through their skin and overhandling can kill them. Watch how they are working hard to turn the soil, mixing in organic matter, air, and water and making it fertile.

SCAVENGER HUNT

A fun and instructive game for a wet afternoon is an indoor scavenger hunt. Challenge your child to find 10 objects around the house and then name—or draw—the natural resources they were made from. For example, a book (tree), wool sweater (sheep's wool), silk scarf (silkworms), pillow (bird feathers), towel (cotton plant). Set a timer and see whether they can do it faster than you!

SMALL DECISIONS, BIG IMPACT

As campaigner Greta Thunberg famously said: "No one is too small to make a difference." Every little eco-friendly act helps secure the planet's future.

Your may feel that given the scale of the challenges facing our planet, your family's efforts—less than a drop in the ocean—are too small to bother with. Your "carbon footprint" is the amount of carbon dioxide you as an individual generate through your day-to-day living. In the US, the average person's carbon footprint is around 16 tons a year. If every individual reduced this by just 2 tons, that would have a significant impact.

LIFESTYLE CHOICES

You contribute to carbon emissions both at home—when you use gas, oil, or electricity to heat your home, cook, and surf the web—and when you travel by car, motorcycle, bus, train, or plane. Out shopping, too, you increase your carbon footprint. Everything you buy has needed fuel at some stage, whether to create the finished good from the raw material or simply to transport it from the farm or factory.

In the last few decades, we've become used to the idea that we can continually do more, go farther, and go faster. Family life can be busy and demanding, and often a shortage of time makes us forget to turn off the lights or bundle clothes into the tumble dryer instead of line drying them.

Every thoughtful little action helps the environment—as do bigger undertakings, such as improving your insulation to heat your home with less fuel and switching to more environmentally friendly sources of power. Twenty percent of US emissions come from households, primarily from housing and transportation.

If you have a car, taking a chunk out of your morning to walk your child to school may seem crazy, especially if you need to be at your own desk straight afterward. Bikes, scooters, or a walking bus can help. You may find chatting with your child on the move is less stressful than fighting traffic as you drive. The more lifestyle swaps you make—for example, by vacationing locally or going by train instead of by airplane—the more a considered pace will start to seem normal, to both you and your child.

FOOD CHOICES

Whether you're a two-person household or a family of seven, it's likely that you spend a lot of time planning and preparing meals. Your food choices, as you raise the next generation, can have an immediate and long-term impact on climate change. When you select local produce rather than out-of-season fruits flown in from abroad, you save on airfreighting. By avoiding products with palm oil in them, or soy grown in a rain forest zone, you help reduce demand for these crops that contribute toward deforestation.

Reducing the amount of dairy and meat you consume, particularly beef and lamb, or (even better) moving fully to a plant-based diet, also helps the environment. The world's population has grown from 2 billion in 1930 to 7.8 billion in 2020. Livestock to feed all these extra mouths requires ever more land to be cleared for grazing or growing animal feed. Cows emit methane (a greenhouse gas) as they digest their food.

Becoming vegetarian or cutting out dairy products may seem unimaginable to some, especially those who have a partner or children wedded to meat-based meals. Many committed vegans started small, for example, by eating red meat just once a fortnight, or by bulking out a meat sauce with lentils. Provided a vegan diet is well planned (particularly for pregnant women, babies, and children) to ensure it incorporates essential nutrients, such as calcium, iron, and vitamin B12, it can supply everything your body needs.

DR ANNABELLE HUMANES

ON OUR BIKES

Since moving to Germany 10 years ago, my family has adopted "green" lifestyle habits that are taken for granted in our new community. Inspired by what we see around us, we rely on our car much less than we used to, even though we now have young children. A bike trailer or cargo bike is considered an essential piece by many expectant parents here, and children cycle to school or kindergarten from as young as two years old. Whether on their own balance bike or in a trailer attached to their parents' bike, they will be on two wheels from spring to winter.

We've also gotten into the habit of spending our leisure time in the open air, come rain or snow. Spending time outdoors, whether in playgrounds or in nature, has been demonstrated to make people engage in more environmentally sustainable behaviors. Our small lifestyle adjustments feel impactful when we see others doing the same.

JEN PANARO

BETTER BIRTHDAYS

Growing up, my family always celebrated birthdays but never in a lavish way. We had small birthday parties as kids that eventually faded with age. Most birthday celebrations happened over a handful of candles and homemade dessert, a few gifts from our parents, and a short rendition of "Happy Birthday." Then we headed off to finish homework.

Despite the low-key celebrations, I never felt like I missed out. In fact, I've embraced simple birthday parties and do the same with our kids. We always share cake and candles, but we waited to host birthday parties for our kids until they were old enough to request them.

Now they invite a few friends to our home and play outside while the parents socialize. We emphasize that guests' presence is more important than presents. We choose reusable serving dishes over single-use alternatives and often schedule between meals to keep the festivities even simpler.

A couple of times, we borrowed a bounce house from friends instead of buying one ourselves. Sharing resources builds the fabric of our community and saved us several hundred dollars. Unsurprisingly, the borrowed bounce house was the biggest hit of any birthday party.

> *"We traded goodie bags for bulk candy in brown paper takeaway bags and used reusable plates."*

Simple and low-waste birthday parties will not change the world alone, but our small actions add up and spark conversation. Requesting that guests not bring gifts reinforces to others and our children that we already have abundance. Having a compost bucket in plain view at a birthday party gave us a chance to explain to friends why we made such choices.

Our small decisions create ripple effects and encourage others to make sustainable living choices, too.

JAMES MURRAY

DRIVING CHANGE

We all live in an era of hyper-connectivity, where purchasing a pack of cookies or new T-shirt is the proverbial beating butterfly's wing that results in the hurricane half a hemisphere away of a felled rain forest or child factory worker.

It is only through an act of willful blindness that we can ignore how our daily decisions contribute to climate change and plastic pollution, to name just two obvious crises. Equally, trying to live a low-impact life within a high-impact society can be paralyzing. Even "green" products can have unintended consequences, and most of the world's biggest problems are systemic, meaning that unless you move completely off-grid, there's always a degree of culpability. (I tend to regard the oft-quoted statistic that 100 companies are responsible for 71 percent of global greenhouse gas emissions as somewhat disingenuous. Those 100 companies operate within an economic system where a lot of customers are buying what they are selling.)

Navigating this complexity becomes harder still when you throw children into the mix. You don't want to give a child hang-ups about the damage we all do to the world, nor do you want to make them overtly judgmental of others' choices. Equally, you have to help prepare them for the world as it is, not how we wish it might be. At the same time, if every new generation is simply plugged into unsustainable systems and behaviors, then catastrophe beckons.

> **"Eating less meat, choosing green businesses—these small actions can help drive systemic change."**

A friend of mine who works as an environmental campaigner has a handy five-point guide for the inevitable "What can I do?" question: 1) eat less meat and dairy, 2) fly less, 3) change to a greener energy supplier, 4) change your bank, and 5) change your pension provider. He also stresses that you should let companies know why you are switching your custom.

These small actions that we can take as parents have positive effects well beyond their direct environmental impacts, by normalizing more sustainable behaviors. Eating less meat, walking and cycling wherever possible, using your purchasing power to reward green businesses, reusing and recycling materials, minimizing the use of plastic, growing some of your own food— all of these are good, healthy, and rewarding choices in and of themselves, but they also help drive the systemic change that can deliver a more sustainable economy for all. It is clearly the case that children play a crucial role in normalizing these new behaviors because that is how generational change has always happened.

How, though, do you encourage children to take positive, green actions themselves? A didactic approach is unlikely to work— children know better than most that rules are there to be broken. The answer has to be to provide

context, to empower children to see how small, responsible actions fit into a bigger picture.

This is an area where culture in general, and children's TV in particular, can help. When I was growing up, kids' TV was limited to teaching you the difference between a circle and a square. Now our kids learn about recycling and marine plastic and renewables and global supply chains simply by watching cartoons. Our five-year-old even has a book about how palm oil contributes to deforestation. These seem like big topics for children, but communicated right they simply help establish responsible patterns of behavior and demonstrate how individual actions can and do add up to help tackle planetary-scale problems.

The US environmentalist Margaret Mead once observed that you should "never doubt that a small group of thoughtful, committed citizens can change the world; indeed, it's the only thing that ever has." The line has become such a touchstone for environmental activists that it is now the stuff of cliché, but that does not make it less true. Everything is connected.

ACTION PLAN
Eat Well

By adjusting your family's diet to a planet-friendly one, you normalize a new way of eating for the next generation. This is vital if the whole of humanity is to be fed as the world's population grows.

BUY ORGANIC

Pesticides and chemical fertilizers are harmful for wildlife, water, soil, and sometimes human health, too. If shopping exclusively organic is too expensive, prioritize some of the worst offenders—those store-bought foods that often contain a cocktail of pesticide residues, such as grapefruit, clementines, strawberries, and lemons.

FOOD DETECTIVES

Challenge your child, either at home or in the supermarket, to see how many products they can find that contain palm oil. They will need to read the ingredients lists on the packaging carefully. Ask for ideas on how you can avoid purchasing those products in the future.

TELL A STORY

Once upon a time, there was a little carrot tucked up snug beneath the ground on a sunny spot on the farm. Does your child know where the food on their plate has come from? Have they seen sheep grazing in fields or apples on a tree, either in pictures or real life? Talk to them about where food comes from.

SWAP AROUND

Reduce the amount of dairy your family consumes day to day with some handy swaps. If you're making sweet treats, one mashed banana can replace one egg in a brownie or cake recipe, to bind the mixture. Or try a tablespoon of applesauce (unsweetened). At breakfast time, offer up oat milk for the morning cereal instead of cow's milk. A recipe of creamy pasta can be made using nuts instead of cheese or cream—cashew nut-based recipes work well, for example.

MAKE PANCAKES

Introduce your child to the joys of cooking healthy, planet-friendly, and delicious food. Blueberry pancakes (using oat milk and banana) topped with maple syrup can be fun to make together any day of the year.

EAT WHOLE

One way to reduce the impact of livestock on the planet is to eat lesser-known cuts. It saves you money, too. Eating the whole animal makes it go further and hold more value for the farmer. Offal is very nutritious, and some children enjoy liver, which can be tender to eat. Pâtés and bone broths are also child-friendly. "Eat whole" works for vegetables, too—there is no need to discard broccoli stems or cauliflower leaves, which can be roasted or stir-fried just like other leafy greens.

PUT BACK WHAT YOU TAKE OUT

Show your child how to give back as well as take and how to be a careful consumer. This will improve their relationship with the planet—and with fellow citizens, too.

Over 12,000 years ago, our hunter-gatherer ancestors lived in small communities and hunted, foraged, and fished from land and sea, taking no more than either could reproduce. We are now far removed from that nomadic existence; however, we need to rediscover the principle of not overexploiting our planet's resources.

SUSTAINABLE LIVING

Sustainability means putting back when you take out. Some companies do this by sponsoring tree-planting programs to offset their energy usage. You may not be able to plant a tree, but your family can still give back. Perhaps you could feed the birds in winter. If there's litter in the park, be the person to pick it up and dispose of it appropriately. Consider donating time or money to a local or national environmental charity such as World Wildlife (WWF). You could even inspire your child to join or help set up an eco club at their school.

The more we reduce our consumption at the outset, the less we need to put back. Two or more gallons of water standardly flow from a tap each minute—so remind your child to turn the tap off when brushing their teeth. Use only the water you need when boiling the kettle and cooking vegetables. Turn your thermostat down one or two degrees to save money as well as the planet. If you're streaming a video on your phone, use less energy by switching to standard definition instead of high (HD).

ZERO WASTE

Garbage pollutes both water and land. Ink or chemicals from junked goods can seep into the soil and harm plants and animals. Plastic is a synthetic material that's been in common use since the 1950s. Its manifold uses in industry, from health care to food storage to renewable energies, make it a force for good. However, discarded single-use plastic clogs our oceans, and even plastic that has been recycled eventually ends up as microplastic particles that can enter our waterways, killing seabirds and fish. Think of every piece of packaging as precious and see how often you can reuse it before recycling it. Even better, aim for zero waste.

Some routes to zero waste are straightforward—reusable water bottles and coffee cups, a packaging-free vegetable box program. Others require a change of attitude, for example, treasuring and repairing household items and shopping for fewer, longer-lasting items.

JEN PANARO

GIVE AND TAKE

One Wednesday afternoon, not long before the holidays approached, I contemplated what we would do with our boys over the break. I popped online and began to search for the perfect jigsaw puzzle but had little luck. Not surprisingly, the majority of results directed me to mediocre options from the seemingly omnipresent retailer that appears at the top of so many online shopping queries.

The search for this elusive puzzle gave me pause, for which I am grateful. The extra moments to reflect on my otherwise impulsive purchase reminded me to seek out the abundance already present in my community. Instead of buying something new, I posted a request in my local Buy Nothing group.

The Buy Nothing project is an international movement to foster hyper-local gifting communities that help reduce consumption and waste while building the fabric of our neighborhoods.

Local groups are independently facilitated within the framework of the Buy Nothing guiding principles. After spending mere months in my local group, I've gifted countless items to others and received a few special items as well.

On this particular wintry Wednesday, I requested a 300-piece jigsaw puzzle. Within a couple of hours, another member offered up a puzzle she no longer needed. By day's end, I had three perfect puzzles. I needn't wait for two-day shipping but instead received new-to-me puzzles within a few hours. My son was stoked.

Gifting economies and sharing communities, much like Mother Nature, function sustainably only when we put back what we take out. While I've received many wonderful gifts from this community, I've also passed along countless things that we have outgrown. We gifted a bed and a mattress, outdoor recreational toys, home organization tools, and so much more, all to families excited to treasure our trash.

Beyond closing the resource loop to ensure that we give as much as

we take, we do our best to reuse and repurpose what we already have. I especially enjoy finding creative ways to reuse items designed for single use. We plant seedlings in yogurt containers and store homemade snacks in repurposed bread bags. We even turned an empty vinegar bottle into a sugar canister.

"I received three new-to-me puzzles within just a few hours—and we didn't have to pay a penny."

Low-waste living doesn't have to be locked at home. Our habits travel with us when we vacation. Initiatives like ShareWaste, a community-based composting platform, enable anyone to compost if they have a host near their home or travel destination. While on vacation recently, we used the ShareWaste app to find a nearby compost host to ensure that the scraps of our meals found their way to the soil.

I want to lead by example for my children, helping them appreciate and make the most of all we have.

JESS PURCELL

REFUSE, REUSE, RECYCLE

No matter how hard we try, our household creates waste. From the packaging on our food to the leftovers we don't eat, to envelopes, boxes, and bottles—waste is inevitable. When we cannot refuse the goods that enter our home, our family strives to be creative and reuse or recycle everything!

Take leftovers. My kids know that their apple cores and banana peels go into the compost container under the sink. And food scraps aren't the only thing we compost— brown paper, egg cartons, newspaper, and cardboard go in, too. By actively participating in taking the food container outside to our compost pile and helping me aerate the heap, they've learned that composting is nature's recycling system.

Although they're a bit young to understand the chemistry of composting, they do recognize the difference between "browns" and "greens." Carbon-rich materials are commonly referred to as "browns" and include such things as dried leaves, cardboard, wood shavings, and newspaper. Nitrogen-rich materials are known as "greens" and include fruit and vegetable scraps, grass clippings, and coffee grounds. They also know that to avoid the compost getting smelly, we have to add air by turning the pile over, which has led to great discussions about the beneficial microbes that reside in the soil.

> *"Composting is nature's recycling system, helping us transform leftovers into rich, fertile soil."*

As well as prompting talks about how we are returning nutrients to the soil, our composting has also opened up conversations about how we are avoiding sending this waste to a landfill or incinerator. We've talked about how the environment in a landfill isn't aerated like our compost pile, and so different microbes are at work to break down the waste. Those microbes create different gases than the oxygen-breathing ones in our backyard, including some that are very harmful to the planet, such as methane. Their young minds can comprehend these basics, which have heightened their curiosity as to what is living in the soil!

Reuse is always a better option than recycling, especially when it comes to plastic. Unfortunately, due to the chemical composition of plastic resins, most plastic packaging can be recycled only once or twice. More often than not, it is actually downcycled into a material that will not be able to be recycled at all once discarded. At the grocery store with my children, I explain why I choose to purchase a slightly more expensive product that is packaged in a glass bottle over a plastic bottle, or why I avoid purchasing certain snacks wrapped in single-use plastic. Explaining to them that plastic never truly goes away and that every piece of plastic ever created still exists sends a strong message, and one that I hope will help guide their purchasing decisions in the future.

Our annual trip to the beach in the summer solidifies that message.

As they walk along the sand and pick up bits of plastic wrappers and bottle caps with me, they are visibly disgusted by the trash that litters their vacation spot. Not only do the plastics themselves invade every aspect of our environment, from microplastics in ocean water to littering our natural spaces, the processes of extracting crude oil and producing plastics release numerous chemicals into the surrounding environments, negatively affecting all nearby life.

Thankfully, innovators and scientists have been working to create some replacement materials for traditional plastics. They are known as bioplastics and are made from plants instead of petroleum. At first glance, these bioplastics have the same structural integrity of traditional plastics; however, when exposed to a composting environment, they will decompose. My kids and I have been experimenting with home snack wrappers that are made of bioplastic in our compost pile, keeping track of how long it takes them to decompose. There are science lessons to be learned in all sorts of places, if only you take the time to look!

ACTION PLAN
Use It Up

Show your child how to make the most of what you have, and involve them, too, in repairing, repurposing, refurbishing, reusing, and remaking!

CHOOSE WOODEN TOYS

Plastic toys can be very eye-catching, but try to buy sustainably sourced wooden toys wherever you can. They tend to last much longer, and once your child has finished with them, they can be passed to a charity store or treasured by friends' children—or even grandchildren eventually! They will also biodegrade when they have finally outlived their usefulness.

JUNK MODEL

Paint a shoebox red and it's a fire truck; a bottle and some sand become a musical instrument; drink cartons can be transformed into skyscraper offices for hardworking dolls; egg cartons make fearsome dragons; and toilet paper roll puppet families can breed faster than rabbits!

BE CRAFTY

Teaching your child to knit, sew, or crochet—and/or basic electronics if that's more where their interests lie—will introduce them to the art of making and also mending. If you can't teach them yourself, perhaps there is a relative who could help, or you could use a book or YouTube videos to learn together.

PLAN MEALS

Most food waste comes from households, not restaurants. Planning meals so you buy only what you need will help reduce waste, as will serving smaller portions—let children ask for second helpings. Use your senses of smell, taste, and sight to judge whether food is still edible beyond its "best before" date. Learn to love leftovers; safely store and reheat them. If you are eating out, be bold about asking for a doggie bag to take home any excess.

CARE FOR CLOTHES

Teach your child to hang their clothes up after each wear so they don't need washing as often. When clothes shopping, consider purchasing one expensive item that will last rather than several cheap ones—natural fibers wear best. For growing children, hand-me-downs, clothes swaps, and thrift stores are your friends.

MAKE A COMPOST HEAP

Ready to try composting yourself? You will need a plentiful supply of "greens" and "browns" (see p.40). For an open-air compost system, clear a 3 sq ft (1 sq m) of ground to bare soil and then fence around it. Make the front wall lower than the rest. Lay twigs or straw on the soil, and then add equal amounts of greens and browns. Turn the mixture regularly with a shovel to aerate it, and keep it covered and moist. Alternatively, a rotating compost tumbler is user-friendly and requires less space.

GROW YOUR OWN

Let your child experience a direct connection with the soil your food comes from by growing something of their own, however small.

Harvesting food to eat that you have grown yourself is magical. It's also an ideal way for children to learn that different types of plants thrive in different soils and climates and that there is a seasonality to what we eat. Food you've grown yourself doesn't need packaging or transporting, nor does it require pesticides or chemical fertilizers that pollute the environment.

SLOW FOOD

The time it takes to produce just a few strawberries or tomatoes can be a shock to anyone used to grabbing what they need for supper from the supermarket shelf. The leisurely pace of production helps your child value the food on their plate. Grow cress in an eggshell or a broad bean plant in a jar, and let them relish the slow, unfolding drama as the plant grows and the produce gradually appears.

You don't need a huge outside space to cultivate useful edibles. Potatoes can be grown in compost bags. Herbs from a window box can transform your meals. Creating a vegetable patch is a fantastic project with your older child if you have a garden. Or if that feels too ambitious, just rewild a little area to attract butterflies, bees, and other pollinators.

JESS PURCELL

GARDEN KNOW-HOW

I've discovered with my kids that growing our own vegetables and herbs is a terrific way to instill in them an appreciation for food and the soil that nourishes it. We enjoy planning our garden each year.

So how do you get started? First and foremost, find a spot of soil. This could be in your backyard, in pots on a balcony, or a plot in a community garden. Once you've determined the area you have to work with, you'll want to ensure that the soil is healthy. Although much of what makes soil fertile cannot actually be seen with the naked eye, there are visual clues. Soil that is dark brown, well aerated, and moist is likely to contain the necessary ingredients.

What are those necessary, unseen ingredients, you might ask? Chemical compounds containing nitrogen, carbon, phosphorus, and potassium are all essential for soil health as well as plant growth. Luckily, all of these essential elements can be found in compost!

Next, you'll need to decide what you want to plant and when. This can be done by simply researching the growing zone you are in. You can also find this information on the back of seed packets; there's usually a map that indicates when particular plants can be sown based on your geographical location. If you're growing your plants from seed, you'll also want to read whether germination should be started indoors and, if so, when it is best to transplant the seedlings outside. Also pay attention to how much sunlight and water each plant needs and whether it will require support, such as lattices or poles to climb.

> *"Sunlight, water, and soil full of air and rich with nutrients will help your plants grow."*

In my experience, when children see the work that goes into tending to plants, less food is wasted at the table as they appreciate the fruits of their labors!

JEN PANARO

PIZZA TOPPINGS

Each year, as winter melts into spring, I dig into my seed collection and plan our summer food garden. My younger son loves to help plant seeds and take care of the garden.

I wanted to give him a little section of the garden to himself, to take ownership and be responsible. He has a pollinator garden area he loves, full of "Tuscan Sun" false sunflowers and lavender, but he yearned for something that required more active management. He also loves harvesting fresh food from our garden.

He was thrilled when we decided to create a pizza garden for him. His pizza garden included a variety of vegetables and herbs we could harvest to make our very own pizzas (or at least sauce and toppings). We planted tomatoes and a variety of herbs like basil and parsley for a homemade one-pot pizza sauce. We also planted peppers, spinach, and eggplant as pizza toppings.

Conveniently, fresh herbs complement tomato plants. Herb aromas help deter curious bugs from exploring sprouting tomato vines. Often in nature, things that we eat together grow well together, too. It never ceases to amaze me how life in nature makes so much sense.

"We planted tomatoes, herbs, and veggies for a nutritious homemade pizza sauce and fresh toppings."

In a world where humans are increasingly distant from our food sources and our impact on the food supply, our pizza garden helps my boys connect with our food.

Edible home gardens bring us one step closer to filling our table with fresh food and connecting our nutritional needs with the bounty of a healthy ecosystem. Introducing our children to the pleasure of digging in the soil and snacking on fruit from the vine leads them down a path to respecting and protecting the land on which we live.

ACTION PLAN
Plant a Seed

Even if the results are modest, discovering the power and potential of the soil will teach your child more about how our planet works and fire their imagination.

HAIRY CATERPILLAR

Wash and dry some eggshell halves and make a caterpillar. Your child might like to study photos and paint the shells a realistic color and make playdough feet. Pop damp cotton balls inside each shell, then sprinkle with cress seeds. Place the caterpillar somewhere sunny and keep the cotton balls moist. After a week, he'll be hairy! Enjoy the cress in a sandwich or salad.

COMMUNITY GARDEN

Find out whether there is a community garden in your area or a group that greens up local spaces, such as the bus or railroad station, and volunteer to do some digging or watering with your child.

JUNK GARDEN

A reluctant young gardener might enjoy making a junk garden, and it's a great way to put odds and ends lying around the home to good use, for example, a pair of worn-out boots. Fill the toe of each boot with gravel or broken-up polystyrene and then top up with compost. Try planting mint or impatiens.

KITCHEN GARDEN

Many herbs can be grown indoors as well as outdoors, allowing your child to become familiar with their fragrance, as well as their taste, as it floods the kitchen. If you have a sunny south-facing window, you could try growing rosemary, thyme, or basil. For a cooler spot by an east-facing window, try mint, parsley, or chives, which need less light. If you've no suitable windowsill, you could consider buying a grow light to help your plants thrive. Make your child responsible for watering their favorite herb.

BE WILD

We cannot survive without insects. Work with your child to plant some flowers in a window box or your garden for the bees, hoverflies, moths, and butterflies to pollinate. The more varied the mixture, the better. If you have outdoor space, don't hesitate to leave a corner wild.

MUD PIES

All human life depends on soil. It contains the nutrients for crops and vegetation to grow, houses bacteria and fungi vital for the production of everything from cheese to penicillin, absorbs rainwater to prevent flooding, and stores carbon, keeping it out of the atmosphere. Encourage your child to explore and play with mud— either outdoors (appropriately dressed) by a stream or puddle, or perhaps in the form of clay modeling.

BE A FRIEND

Global citizenship starts in the playground. By showing children how to embrace differences, we enable them to forge rich and rewarding friendships.

FRIENDSHIP VALUES

The quality of our relationships has a profound impact on our lifelong happiness and mental health. Help your child develop the values they need to create meaningful bonds.

Young children are naturally open-minded, and you have the power to help your child develop into a loving, caring person capable of fulfilling friendships that transcend boundaries of place or identity. By regularly responding to them with empathy and compassion, you give them the tools to treat other people in the same way. This starts at a very young age as they engage with family members and then other children at day care or playgroup.

COMPASSIONATE CARE

When a human cares about a person in distress, brain scans show that part of the lower brain lights up. A caregiver who responds with love and attention to a baby's needs is helping them form vital connections in their brain that will allow them to be compassionate and empathetic. This crucial social intelligence—something that children learn rather than are born with—enables them to form rewarding friendships.

Listening to your child, helping them find the words to express their feelings, and demonstrating to them that you understand the strong emotions they are experiencing will all improve their capacity to interact positively with others. With a very young child, this might mean that instead of insisting they "be good" and let another child play with their toy, you acknowledge to them that it makes them feel angry to have to share and together find a way to do it that they can accommodate.

VIVE LA DIFFÉRENCE

Your child's school will likely have people with a wide variety of beliefs and family backgrounds. This is a great place to start learning how to be a friend with someone who experiences life differently from you. Encourage respectful curiosity in your child about their classmates' views and identities—and accept this as a two-way experience. A good friend will challenge your assumptions as well as respect your beliefs.

Does your child know what it feels like to not belong, to be overlooked, or to be misunderstood? It's probable that everybody has experienced this feeling at some point. How does it feel to live that all the time, as so many children do who don't quite fit society's perceived norms? Something as simple as donning a blindfold to eat breakfast can give you both an instant insight into what it feels like to be visually impaired, for example, building empathy. If you show tolerance and open-mindedness, your child is likely to imbibe those values.

DR MELERNIE *MEHEUX*

MODEL CITIZENS

I've always enjoyed friendships, interacting, and connecting. When training as an educational psychologist, I discovered friendships weren't just rewarding but essential for human development. Good friendships promote mental health and prepare children to navigate adulthood and be good citizens. It's important in today's interconnected world that we instill in children the values they need for happy friendships.

The first friendship values are instilled as early as infancy, before a child can even speak. Empathy and trust are the first values you teach as a parent, perhaps without even knowing, which is why psychologists talk about the criticality of early years development.

Donald Winnicott spoke about "good enough" parenting shaping development. "Good enough" parental responses to a baby crying are ones that teach them

that their needs will always be met. When a parent figures out what a cry means, and provides a feed or a change, their baby becomes calmer, and a process starts that psychologists call "attunement." This means that a caregiver knows exactly how to soothe the baby— the baby trusts them and feels safe. All this happens without conscious understanding or discussion.

> **"Parents are a child's first role models, unconsciously teaching them behaviors and values."**

As the child grows up, these interactions continue. Thus, the child learns that relationships will meet their needs and are important for survival. This also leads to the manifestation of these values within the child's own friendships.

Parents and carers are our first role models. We inadvertently "teach" the behaviors and values we want to see in children. Interactions with family members, friends, and the world around us are lessons for children. Being patient, communicating openly, and showing respect for others and our environment are all important. Showing we can express views while listening and valuing different opinions is key to developing children's communication and problem solving. Thus, we teach children it's possible to forgive, accept differences in others, and remain friends.

Encouraging and supporting play is one of the best ways of developing children's friendship values. Prior to becoming a psychologist, as a teacher, I saw how play developed sharing, taking turns, and feelings of community and connectedness. Being West African, we had lots of gatherings with family and friends, which provided regular play opportunities, including rough and tumble play, role play, and board games. It was an integral part of childhood, teaching me that friendship, belonging, and connection were the building blocks of human life.

I must stress the importance of allowing children to make choices about who they want to be friends with. It is imperative we teach children it is okay to be open to a range of friendships. We can model this through our own friendships and the language we use when talking about people who live alongside us in our communities or that we see on television, who may outwardly appear different from us. We need to affirm that it is okay if our friends do not look like us, talk like us, or learn in the same way as us, or if their bodies move in different ways from ours. We must be inclusive and open to positive feelings of friendship with anyone, irrespective of any differences, and challenge others who don't do the same.

The digital divide, inequality, and difference within our communities are often instantly visible when we turn on the television or walk around our towns and cities. It's important to have discussions about what we see in front of us and stories we read in newspapers or on the internet about human beings, animals, or groups who are disadvantaged or being treated unfairly. Through our conversations, we can teach compassion, understanding, and respect for the world, other cultures, faiths, and communities. This, too, is vital for secure friendships.

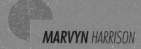

MARVYN HARRISON

LETTING GO

From the first time you wave goodbye to your children and watch them disappear beyond their school gates, your parenting changes. Suddenly, you can't stop thinking about the people your children will allow into their lives and whether or not you've molded them into good enough humans to even make friends. Although it's relatively easy for kids to make friends at that early stage, the meaningful children's relationships develop a lot sooner than you expect.

From about seven years old and beyond, children develop a clearer view of who they want to be friends with. Phrases like "they are not my friend" and "they are my best friend" become fundamental for them. What might not be as obvious, though, is that your children's relationships will be directly influenced by the ways you interact with them and others around them. As our children's very first friends, we can only hope that we've given them best lessons in

friendship. Do I use enough manners around them? Am I kind to strangers? Am I honest?

Once your children begin forming real relationships, the key thing to consider is that their friends' behavior will likely mirror their own. So if your kids are spending time with the "cool kids" who often disrupt class, ask yourself why. If their friends are kindhearted and share similar interests with them, ask yourself why, too.

This can't simply be boiled down to *my child is good* or *my child is bad*. Instead of monitoring their friendships, focus on who they're becoming as people.

First off, make sure they know what their values are—whether that's as simple as doing their homework or as complex as caring about the less fortunate—and make sure they understand how those values will apply in different situations.

Second, make sure they're true to those values. No matter the age, that part is imperative to make real connections.

This is also the point where your kids start developing their own individuality. When it comes to friendships, you don't want your kids to get swallowed up. Instead of seeking acceptance from their friends or giving in to peer pressure, you want them to be able to recognize (and avoid) unhealthy behavior. If your children are unclear about which behaviors are unhealthy, they could end up dealing with toxic friends who leave them open to making bad decisions—which could have a long-term impact.

If you want to understand your children's friends, try connecting with their parents. This allows for an insight into their parenting style, culture, and discipline, and why your children may have attracted each other. At the end of the day, you can't control who your children befriend, but there are ways to get a sense of your children's friendships as part of the bigger picture. Being a global citizen means that your child understands different cultures, has a strong sense of empathy, and builds respectful relationships not only with their friends but with the people who surround their friends, too.

There's a tool I like to use with my eldest child, to teach him about meaningful friendships. I call it the "Who will you be?" scenarios. This tool works for children of all ages and allows them to understand the consequences of real-life interactions.

"You can't control who your child befriends, but you can ensure they know and are true to their values."

Try asking your child these questions and see how they answer. Is there anything important to teach them about friendship through their answers?
- Who will you be if **your friend is mean to you?**
- Who will you be if **your friends laugh at you?**
- Who will you be if **your friends don't share?**
- Who will you be if **your friends ask you to do something you don't want to do?**
- Who will you be if **you upset your friend intentionally?**
- Who will you be if **you irritate your friend unintentionally?**

ACTION PLAN
Trust and Respect

Help your child develop empathy, trust, respect, and compassion so that they are able to be a good friend, and show them how healthy relationships look and feel.

BE SMART

If your child struggles to know how to handle a challenging relationship, talk to them about the different ways they could react to their friend. Help them figure out what a kind response looks like, and then ask them about a brave response, a smart one, a powerful one, a loving one, and a thoughtful one. What does this tell them about what they need to do?

PLAYDATES

Encourage your child to host and go on playdates so that they have the opportunity to develop friendships. It will also give you an opportunity to observe how they interact with their friends and where they might need help learning the best way to treat or be treated by a friend. Talk openly about any difficulties.

GOOD MANNERS

Good manners are more than "please" and "thank you." Showing good manners to a friend needn't mean formal language, but it should mean showing them respect, by taking their views seriously and being thoughtful. Show your child good manners so that they do the same with you and others.

GAME NIGHT

Pop the popcorn and close the curtains—it's family game night! As well as fostering a sense of belonging and connectedness, games are a fantastic way for children to learn to take turns, respect rules, and feel empathy for the loser. Strategy board games such as Monopoly can improve their problem-solving and negotiation skills. Invite another family over to double the fun and keep everyone on their best behavior! A bingo night can work for all ages.

PUT ON A SHOW

Getting into character for a dramatic performance is a great way to put yourself in somebody else's shoes—literally. Encourage your children to create and put on a play or a concert, with you as their audience. This will teach them the art of cooperation and compromise, too.

SAY SORRY

Sometimes we worry that admitting wrongdoing to our children might undermine our authority, but everyone makes mistakes; the important thing is how we deal with this. If you behave unreasonably, say "sorry" to your child, and articulate what you did wrong and how you should have behaved. This will give them a model for their own behavior.

IDENTITY MATTERS

How do you see yourself? How would you like your child to see themselves? Help them become comfortable with their own story and celebrate other people's.

Your child is growing up in a society where a broad range of beliefs, behaviors, and identities is the norm. Whereas in the past a classroom may have been made up of children from families with similar, ingrained attitudes, easier travel and the internet have broken down barriers this century. Awareness of differences does not guarantee acceptance, however.

GENDER AND RELATIONSHIPS

Attitudes to sexual relationships and gender have changed since today's parents were born. A General Social Survey, based on data from 1977 to 2016, found that most Americans believe women should have equal roles at work; however, nearly 25 percent of those surveyed think women should still take on a bigger role at home, such as household chores and child-rearing. Although more women are doing paid work outside of the home, they are still responsible for the majority of domestic duties, and men have not necessarily taken on more domestic work.

Attitudes toward same-sex relationships have also changed significantly over the past 15 years. According to the Pew Research

Center, a poll in 2004 found that the majority of Americans opposed same-sex marriage. Now those numbers are reversed, with 61 percent of Americans in support of same-sex marriage, although that means a significant minority are still against it. Tolerance of prejudice and actual discrimination against the LGBTQ+ community is widespread in some circumstances. Attitudes toward transgender, where people change the sex they were assigned at birth through lifestyle actions and/or medication or surgery, are particularly complex, with many people not considering themselves prejudiced yet not totally clear that transphobia is always wrong.

RACE AWARE

In a world where the school curriculum frequently offers a very narrow perspective on our history and culture, and where teachers can be constrained by government guidance in the ways they discuss and teach race, parents of all colors have a vital role to play in opening their child's eyes to structural racism. This racism can be hard to spot. It's people with the same biases joining together, even unconsciously, to act in ways that assume whiteness is the norm and which diminish the views,

life chances, opportunities, and experiences of people of color. It's still rare for Black, Asian, or minority ethnic teachers to be on school leadership teams, even in those schools that do have a diverse staff. While all children are born equal, not all are listened to or supported equally by adults. Help your child hear, respect, and validate other children's points of view.

I AM SPECIAL BECAUSE

Whether your child feels different because of their gender, sexual orientation, ethnicity, religion, special needs or disability, their socioeconomic status relative to their classmates, or any other reason—maybe simply the color of their hair—encourage them to love who they are. You can play a version of the circle-time activity "I am special because" at home. Ask them to tell you what makes them unique—their interests as well as their talents—and they can ask you to do the same. Incorporate this sense of having something to offer the world into your conversation on a regular basis. The more secure they feel, the less they will experience a need to call out others for their differences and instead can help foster a warm, supportive environment around them.

FARIBA SOETAN

PRINCESS LIKE ME

My partner and I are raising three mixed-race daughters in a world where standards of beauty and success, and certain career choices, are predefined by a dominant narrative: often male and most often white.

When my oldest daughter, then four years old, came home wanting to have "vanilla skin" like Mama, despite everything we had taught them, we knew we had our work cut out for us. Even living in a hugely diverse city, the odds were against us in the images they saw, the advertisements, the TV shows (though these are getting better), and our stratified society (the only nonwhite staff member at her school was support staff).

We've learned from experience that representation does matter. And that for our children to know that they, too, can aspire to be a scientist, a CEO, or—more important for my five-year-old—a princess, we have to be intentional about exposing them to more diverse images and media.

If you're just starting out on this journey, you don't need to be an expert. Books can be the most powerful teachers. Take the helpless, white, blonde princess scenario for example. *Princess Grace, Princess Cupcake Jones,* and other series (see Resources, p.216) can expose our children to a different portrayal of what it means to be "royal."

> *"I'll never forget the first time my daughter exclaimed, 'Look, Mama! She looks like me!'"*

So today, when my children draw princesses, they often draw them with brown skin and curly hair, with hands on their hips in fierce defiance—because they have been taught to know that princesses CAN look like them AND be fearless.

If we teach our children to feel good about their differences and to know that they can be themselves, they'll be much better able to deal with whatever life throws at them.

DR ANNABELLE HUMANES

WHERE ARE YOU FROM?

Just like commenting on their cool shirt or dress, asking someone, "Where are you from?" is a very common conversation opener. Some may ask this question because they are genuinely curious and love to discover more about others' stories and backgrounds. Yet the undertone can sometimes feel negative, especially in a context where the questioner has a different accent or skin color from you. It can seem to suggest they think you are not actually from "here." It implies otherness and difference in a less than positive way.

My daughter, now 11 years old, struggles with "where are you from?" As a cross-cultural child, she does not find it offensive, but she finds it extremely difficult to answer and very off-putting. She was born in the UK. She lives in Germany. Her mother is French, and her father is Portuguese.

When well-meaning adults pose this question, she struggles to give the expected and satisfactory one-word reply. We've explored possible brief answers, including saying she is European. This is never what people want to hear and often leads to yet more questions.

I think there are more positive ways of exploring others' stories. My very favorite option is a phrase coined by writer and photographer Taiye Selasi: "Where are you a local?" After all, we rarely have

> **"Asking my daughter where she's from is like asking someone to choose their favorite child."**

a relationship with the whole of a country (a nonnatural political entity). Many would prefer to be asked where they currently live. Another good question is to ask what languages someone speaks, or where they have spent time during their lifetime—or, simply, which place(s) around the world feels like home.

LET FRIENDSHIPS BLOSSOM IN NEW AND UNEXPECTED PLACES.

ACTION PLAN
Celebrate Each Other

Building your child's self-esteem will help them find the good in other people as well as themselves and celebrate who they really are.

DEVELOP INTERESTS

If you look hard enough, you can often find a shared interest with the most unlikely of people. Encourage your child to develop their talents and try out new hobbies. Not only will finding activities they enjoy boost their confidence, but it will give them more opportunities to find points of connection with others.

BE POSITIVE

However frustrating a job half done might be, if you only ever criticize the mess when your child has helped make supper or comment on the forgotten socks when they've "sorted" the laundry, they will get into the habit of focusing on the negatives, too. Acknowledge the good in their efforts before you explain how there's room for improvement.

LET THEM DO IT

Resist the temptation to step in too soon and fix it when your child is struggling to build their brick tower or dress their doll independently. Let them prove to themselves that they can achieve their goal, and each small success will increase their self-esteem and belief in their own capabilities.

SHOW LOVE

To help your child love themselves, make sure they know that you love them, too. Offer meaningful praise when it's due. Teach them that you value the effort they put into something whether or not they succeed. If they misbehave, let them know that it's their behavior you don't like, not them, and you will help them correct it.

BE KIND

Helping other people can transform the way your child feels, making them see themselves as someone who does good in the world whom people like. Involve your child in good deeds you do for neighbors or friends. Let them take note of other people's resilience and appreciate that no one has it easy.

EVERYDAY HEROES

Who are your child's heroes or heroines? See whether you can find some worthy role models, outside the usual run of celebrities. Perhaps they know people at school or in the community who unobtrusively keep clubs and services running. Or log on to the globalcitizen.org website and read about the winners of their "global citizen" awards—men and women who have poured their hearts and souls into making the world a better place.

LOVE LANGUAGE

Knowledge of other languages helps us connect with different cultures. It also enriches the way we think and live our day-to-day experiences.

Did you know that in Turkish, "he," "she," and "it" are all translated by the single, gender-neutral pronoun "o"? Or that there's an Inuit word—*iktsuarpok*—for the feeling of anticipation you have when you wait for someone to visit your house and keep going to check whether they've arrived? Learning even the rudiments of other languages gives children a window into unfamiliar cultures and new ways of thinking.

SPEAK TO MORE PEOPLE

There are approximately 7,000 languages spoken around the world—and more than a billion Mandarin speakers, 637 million Hindi speakers, and 538 million Spanish speakers. Learning one or more of those languages vastly increases the number of people you can connect with! English is the most-spoken language overall; Mandarin Chinese is the most-spoken first language, followed by Spanish, English, Arabic, and Hindi. In the US, which does not have an official language, Spanish or Spanish Creole is the second-most common language after English.

At birth, babies have the potential to speak any language in the world. By 8–12 months, they are focusing in on the sounds spoken around them— that is, their native language, or languages if growing up in a bilingual environment. As they grow older, they lose the ability to distinguish between the sounds that they are not exposed to. The younger children are when learning foreign words and sounds, the better, as until the age of seven or eight, they have the potential to master a foreign language without an accent. Learning one foreign language makes it easier to go on to learn another as well as improving your ability in your native tongue.

COMMUNICATE BETTER

Good communication is a key life skill, enhancing friendships, relationships, and success at work. In our global world, it's normal to mingle with nonnative speakers. Even a slight knowledge of the other person's first language will lead to a greater depth of understanding. At the most simplistic level, the literal translation of "pain au chocolat," for example, as "bread with chocolate," will conjure up a misleading image of the French viennoiserie. Just a "hello" or "thank you" offered in the other speaker's language, especially when traveling, demonstrates a willingness to engage that kick-starts more effective communication.

Research suggests that bilingual children and children who are exposed to another language in their daily lives even have increased empathy. They are better at routinely understanding another person's perspective than monolingual children are. They have also been shown to demonstrate greater creativity and problem-solving skills. Seeing the world through different lenses improves the ability to think in new and fresh ways.

INCREASE CROSS-CULTURAL UNDERSTANDING

Studies have shown that when children learn another language, their attitude toward native speakers of that language becomes significantly more positive. Learning the language of relatives and ancestors can, of course, also help your child have a greater understanding of their heritage. Language learning isn't just grammatical structures and vocabulary; it also teaches you what the norms of the society are and its cultural customs. For example, a businessperson learning English might be taught expressions about the weather to help them make small talk before they get down to brass tacks!

DR ANNABELLE HUMANES

IMMERSE YOURSELVES

Over half of the world's population speaks two or more languages. The benefits of being bilingual are numerous. Some recent studies have found that bilingual children are more tolerant, have better social skills, and have better working memory. They also have better concentration and can switch between tasks more quickly. If your native language differs from the one your child hears around them in the community, knowledge of yours is one of the best gifts you can give them.

Let me reassure you that learning two languages from birth will not confuse or delay your child's language acquisition; children learning two languages will develop within monolingual norms (in terms of speed of learning). Many warn against bilingualism on the basis of stories they've heard about distant acquaintances who were late talkers or ended up speaking only one language. There are also monolingual late talkers, and these anecdotal cases are not supported by scientific research.

Bilingual children may prefer one language over another at some point in time. This is totally natural. I am a bilingual adult. I live in Germany and have a German phone number, yet when I talk to other people in German, I still prefer to give out my phone number in English.

Whether you are teaching your child your own language, or a language you have studied, or one you hope to learn together, the same principles apply.

Start early Babies are able to distinguish between different languages from as young as a few weeks old, and they begin to understand them quite quickly. The earlier you start, the easier it will be—although it is never too late to begin.

Set yourself a goal and be realistic What do you want your child to get out of this exposure to another language? To be able to chat easily to their grandparents in their native tongue, or to succeed in buying an ice cream while on vacation in Italy?

Make it fun You know your child's interests best. Find their favorite book or television show in the target language; some streaming services even allow you to switch language on programs that were made in English originally. When they were little, my own children loved to interact with puppets who could speak "only" Portuguese. One particular puppet used to join us for

> "Surround your child with other languages. The earlier you start, the easier and more natural it will be."

bath time every single day. He stayed for maybe 20 minutes and there was a lot of laughter.

Immerse yourselves Tune in to a different language radio via the internet, connect with speakers from different languages on social media, borrow foreign language books from the library and puzzle over different scripts. Perhaps you know a babysitter who's fluent in another tongue. Multilingual role models, whether that's you or someone else, can bring languages to life and inspire your child.

ACTION PLAN
Learn New Words

Make learning new words and awareness of other languages a part of your everyday family life.

JAMES, JAKOB, IAGO

Find a website that translates names into other languages and let your child discover what their first name is in German, Welsh, or whichever languages pique their interest. They may like you to start referring to them by their new name!

LEARN TO SIGN

Sign language is a visual means of communicating used mainly by those who are deaf or have hearing impairments. It uses gestures and movements of the hand, body, face, and head. Look up American Sign Language online and challenge yourself and your child to learn some signs, perhaps during the school breaks. You never know when it will come in useful.

PLAY A GAME

Give Spot It! or Snap a new twist by playing it in a different language. Together you will need to research and learn the vocabulary for the items displayed on the cards. Shouting out the foreign word instead of the English one when you claim a matching item will soon embed it in both players' brains!

WORD SPOT

Investigate how many foreign words your child is already familiar with. Preschoolers probably know spaghetti and pasta (Italian). School-aged children will be familiar with café, croissant, and ballet (French). Teenagers may have heard of hygge—the Danish word we've adopted for being cozy indoors—or Schadenfreude (German for delight at somebody else's misfortune).

SING OUT

It doesn't matter how well you can hold a tune; singing to your baby and then singing with your child from an early age helps them learn the rhythms and patterns of language. If you are raising your child to be bilingual, lyrics from both languages will reinforce the words they hear spoken.

CIAO, RAGAZZI

Why not introduce some new vocabulary into your everyday routines? You could begin by wishing the family ¡buen provecho! (enjoy your meal, Spanish), as they would in Mexico, before you start eating at dinnertime. You could vary your greeting, too, when you see your child after school. "G'day" might trigger an interesting conversation about how other English-speaking nations use words differently.

TALK ABOUT IT

It's not always easy to find the right words to discuss differences—but your conversations with your child can help them change the debate as they grow up.

In our busy lives as parents, often it's not until something goes wrong that we find the time to address a difficult topic such as bullying or conflict with a friend. Sometimes that's too late, since your child might shut down if they feel overwhelmed by a bad experience. It's worth making a real effort to foster open channels of communication from the get-go, especially if bad experiences of your own, as a child or an adult, mean you find this difficult.

HOW OLD?

Is there an age at which you should actively prompt discussion of a sensitive subject, such as race, gender, or disability? If your child is on the receiving end of an unkind comment when they start school, you may need to do this as young as four. This may feel difficult, particularly if the hurtful comments are ones you yourself can directly relate to. You may feel you want to protect their innocence for as long as you can. On the other hand, if your child is happy in a diverse environment, you may feel there's no need to verbalize their experiences, as you consider your child naturally accepting of others.

The sooner you start having open conversations about tricky topics, the sooner your family gets into good habits around sharing worries, even ones as simple as not knowing what to say to the new girl in class. It's hard for an older child or a teenager at secondary school to suddenly raise concerns about emotive and distressing subjects, such as discrimination or self-harm (even when it concerns a friend, rather than themselves), if as a family you've never found the language or the right forum for these sorts of discussions. A child growing up in a diverse environment can struggle just as much as one in a monocultural environment to articulate their responses to everyday behaviors.

RIGHT MOMENT

For younger children, family mealtimes can be a great place to talk about the issues and concerns of the day. Young children tend to see the world in simple black and white terms; as they grow, you can help them become more nuanced in their thinking. Older children, particularly teenagers, may be more forthcoming one on one, and when the spotlight isn't directly on them—for example, on a trip together somewhere or when you're both distracted, perhaps when doing dishes. The conversations always need to be age appropriate (and what's appropriate will vary with every

child)— but in fact, children often self-select what they hear, shutting out anything you say that they don't feel ready for.

Often the easiest route into a tricky topic—whether that's relationships, prejudice, or something else—can be watching a movie or TV show together and letting conversations arise naturally from your viewing. Your child might be curious as to why a character behaved in a certain way, and you can both unpick the significance. Books can be similarly debated.

Your home is a communal space you control. If your child doesn't see many other children who look or sound or feel like them when they go out into the world, make sure that when they are at home, there are books, toys, pictures, and music around that reflect back at them who they are. Home is their safe space where they can feel grounded and secure in their identity, even if the rest of the world is alien.

Conversely, if your child only ever meets people just like them at school or in the local community, try to diversify your home environment to open their eyes to the wider world. Read a story book whose hero has a disability, for example, and buy the crayon set that has a range of colors to create any skin tone, not just beige or peach. In doing this, you will educate yourself, too.

LISTEN AND SPEAK

Every person—and that includes every child—experiences the world differently. The first step in communicating is active listening. Try to really hear what your child is telling you instead of assuming you understand because of experiences you have had or friends' children have had. Repeat back to them what they have told you so that they know you've taken it in. Listen to your child not just when you have set aside time for a conversation but also day to day as they let little comments slip. If they mention they wish they were different in some way, is that just because they want to be like the heroine of their favorite TV show, or does it stem from judgments made at school? Don't jump to conclusions, but do explore where they are.

Sometimes conversations feel hard because we lack the language. Some terms are nuanced, such as ethnicity (which refers to cultural factors, including nationality, regional culture, ancestry, and language) and race (which refers to skin color, religion, or area of origin). Others are evolving in their use, such as BAME (Black, Asian, and Minority Ethnic), which can offend by the way it lumps together groups that are not a homogenized mass, and by diminishing the status of those whose race actually forms a global majority. However, discomfort at not knowing how to respond can be misinterpreted by your child as disapproval around the topic, leading them to think there is something shameful about what they've said. The simple act of calmly letting them speak, to articulate their questions and confusion, is helpful, before you've uttered a word. You can admit to your child you're not certain of the right way to say something, and investigate this together, explaining that certain words have the power to hurt.

When your child makes a comment that feels inappropriate, a useful question to ask them can be: "What makes you say that?" If they are blindly repeating a generalized stereotype, work with them to interrogate it. Consider people you know, and/or famous people, and explore how each one is an individual. If your child tells you about something that happened at school, you can ask, "How did hearing that make you feel?" Giving children the words they need to express themselves will help them validate their own and others' experiences.

FARIBA SOETAN

TALKING ABOUT RACE

Difference isn't just about some people and not others. Everybody is different, and children as young as two or three start asking about differences, such as disabilities and gender, and physical characteristics like hair and body shape.

These moments are opportunities— a chance to introduce difference to our children, to explore how we're all made in different shapes, colors, and sizes.

My partner and I are raising three mixed-race daughters, and it's important to us that we teach our children to embrace what makes them different, to be confident about it, proud even. Our children know that their brown skin color, their curly hair, and being a girl are all things to celebrate because we've been intentional about talking to them about this since they were born.

Somewhere around four or five years old, children begin to make conscious decisions about who they play with based on things as arbitrary as "he wears glasses" or "she has funny hair." They have already begun to develop unconscious bias based on their idea of what is "normal" in the world around them and started to learn to assign characteristics to certain things.

So children might learn to perceive brown skin as "dirty" or girls as weak or consider the idea that a child with brown skin could be born to a white mother not possible (as was the case with a child in my daughter's class). It's important in these discussions

> *"Our daughters celebrate their gender, their brown skin color, and their curly hair."*

not to scold or shush a child who questions but rather ask them why they might think this, show them images that challenge those assumptions, and gently explain why that is not the case. Talking to children about racism is never going to be comfortable. Although

I was initially alarmed by the child who told me I couldn't be my daughter's mom because I didn't have the same skin color, I realized it was just not in her consciousness that families could look so different. We talked about how each child is a mixture of both parents, and I explained that my daughter's dad was Black and I'm olive-skinned so our children came out a light brown color. She got it. It made sense in her world: color mixing.

If you don't live in a diverse area, try to use books, magazines, TV shows, movies, and ads to introduce diverse characters. Be intentional about seeking out diversity—not simply the books that talk about difference as their main subject but diverse characters doing everyday things. Point out all the similarities, like the fact both characters like playing soccer or wearing hoodies. The differences are there, but they're not more important than what makes them similar.

As children get older, they start to become more discerning about the world around them, questioning why things are the way they are. Part of this shift includes absorbing the not-so-subtle messages of power and privilege surrounding them.

To start a discussion, try talking to them about some of the messages we receive in our everyday lives. Are there particular people who never seem to be the superhero or princess in your books or movies? Those who always seem to "save the day," the ones who need to be "saved," the ones considered "pretty"?

Conversations with my children about race have often spurred ongoing discussions that have branched into gender and class. After so many years of questioning what we see in the media, they know that when there's an ad about a boy playing with LEGO bricks or a girl dressed in pink, we question the message it is giving us.

Failing to talk to children about these important topics means they will go elsewhere to get answers. Admittedly, I don't always get it right, and these discussions will become more difficult over the years. But my children don't have the luxury or privilege of ignoring race. It's through these conversations that our children will begin to understand that difference is good and it's what makes us all special.

ACTION PLAN
Express Feelings

Bottling up how we feel, either about upsetting comments or worries over how to relate to another person, usually makes things worse. Help your child air their concerns in a constructive way.

USE PROPS

Emotion cards (available online from resources such as Twinkl) and picture books can be helpful for naming and discussing feelings. Your child might also have a very nosy teddy bear who always wants to know about their day. A child's play will often give clues to their feeling. If their toys are playing angry, fighting games you might want to explore what's prompted this.

MAKE ART

Children sometimes find it easier to convey how they feel via a drawing or painting than words. Making art together—with clay, papier mâché, or any other material—is also a useful way for them to slowly and calmly process feelings and develop a trusting bond with you so they are comfortable sharing.

RESPECT THEIR EXPERIENCE

Sometimes angry outbursts can be a sign of anxiety in older children, along with negative thoughts, poor concentration, and avoiding everyday activities. Try not to dismiss their worries as trivial or exacerbate them with your own reactions. The CDC website can offer help and advice on anxiety.

ROLE PLAY

Arming your child with some useful vocabulary can make their playground interactions run more smoothly. Handy phrases include "please stop saying that," "it's not okay," and "that didn't sound kind." Have them practice saying these words out loud to you in a role play so that they are confident about using them if the need arises. Help them come up with other ideas as to how they can calmly but assertively articulate what they are thinking.

ASK FOR HELP

If your child struggles to communicate, you may find it valuable to seek support and share your own feelings and concerns. The CDC website is a good starting point for information. If you suspect you have a child on the autism spectrum, try the Autism Speaks website.

PORT IN A STORM

Learning to deal with strong feelings takes time. Encourage your child to bring their emotions to you or to a sympathetic school staff member if they are not able to manage them alone. Sometimes the hurt another child has caused is unintentional, and you can help your child appreciate that a classmate just prefers to play by themselves or has needs your child hasn't understood. Other times your child might need you and their teacher to work calmly together to navigate a difficult situation.

MORE IN COMMON

All humans have the capacity to empathize, to listen to each other, and to see ourselves in the other. Finding our common humanity is a rewarding experience for all ages.

Human beings are born free and equal in dignity and rights—as states the Universal Declaration of Human Rights, adopted by the United Nations in 1948. Children everywhere are born with the same rights as a result of our common humanity. As we help them navigate their way in life, we can guide them to seek common values in unfamiliar places.

FINDING FRIENDS

As Barack Obama said in his first presidential inaugural address: "... we cannot help but believe that ... as the world grows smaller, our common humanity shall reveal itself." Parents the world over want the same things for their children, regardless of their country of origin, religion, skin color, sexuality, or anything else. Keep this in mind as you encourage friendships with families different from your own. Being excited about your child's new classmate will inspire them to follow up on their interest.

If your child's school is not very diverse, consider other ways you can broaden your horizons as a family (see p.86). These activities might not instantly lead to new friendships for your child, but they will show them that we can make connections with citizens from anywhere around the globe.

JESS PURCELL

UNEXPECTED PALS

One aspect of being a high-school teacher that I truly enjoyed was watching unlikely friendships form and blossom. Serving as the teacher representative for my school's community service club, my students and I spent time with primary school students, as well as with elderly citizens at our local retirement home. Witnessing teenagers connect with both younger and older generations was thrilling, as they learned to appreciate both the similarities and differences between themselves and others.

Another good way to build unlikely relationships is through having pen pals. As a young girl, I had pen pals from South Korea, Germany, Greece, France, and Staten Island! I remember being amazed at how someone from across the world liked the same boy band that I did, while at the same time being intrigued by different aspects of their school life. These friendships broadened my perspective on how others lived.

Your child's teacher may be able to recommend pen-pal services, or why not reach out to family, friends, or coworkers who live in a different part of the world? Many schools and community groups have clubs that volunteer their time at retirement facilities, where they meet with residents once or twice a month to do crafts, play games, or help decorate for upcoming events. Your local church may also suggest ways in which your family can make connections with older parishioners and learn from and appreciate a different generational view on current events or topics of interest.

> *"It was thrilling to see appreciation and friendship grow between teenagers and elderly citizens."*

At the core of these unlikely friendships is respect. Building respect for others also builds respect for oneself, as well as an ability to see and appreciate multiple perspectives.

JAMES MURRAY

SHARING STORIES

I always wanted to be a journalist. The combination of writing, public service, and interviewing has never lost its appeal. Although after 20 years, I still find that last part of the job spec nerve-jangling.

People can be wary of journalists, and often with good reason. Some clam up; others respond with hostility. More frequently, they simply fail to answer the question. There are two broad strategies for eliciting information in such a scenario. One is to attack with pointed questions and barely concealed incredulity. It can work, but it typically generates more heat than light. It often makes for good TV and bad journalism.

The alternative is to try to engage, to empathize, to let the conversation flow. There is usually common ground to connect over.

Our boys are at an age—five and three—when they are starting to wrestle with the same challenges I've spent my career trying to navigate. They are no longer little balls of id and are starting to recognize how others have their own feelings and priorities. They are learning the joy of playing with, rather than alongside, others. They are starting to know the value of friendship.

> **"There's almost always common ground. Most people want to share their story, if you are ready to listen."**

Watching this tricky transition is inspiring and upsetting. Their faces can crumple as they try to process the competing desires to hold onto their toy or share with a playmate. They beam when offers of friendship are reciprocated and sob when they are rebuffed. Connecting with people can be hard, whatever age you are.

I'm not ordering the boys their first reporters' notepads, but as their relationships evolve, I'll have some professional as well as fatherly advice. Everyone has a story to share, and in the sharing of those stories, friendships are forged.

ACTION PLAN
Reach Out

Break out of your comfort zone and broaden your family's horizons by engaging with new activities and people that are often hidden in plain sight. This will help you all open up to new friendships.

BE CURIOUS

If a classmate has recently arrived from somewhere new, look up on the map the town or country they've come from and find out all about it. Showing an informed interest will make them feel welcome and make the stories they tell more interesting.

TRY A NEW ACTIVITY

Consider attending a local event that you wouldn't normally engage with, and you might discover a new aspect to your town or city. The library or local park is a good place to start for information on cultural activities and celebrations for different communities in your area, such as music, food, or art festivals or a story-time session.

VENTURE IN

Are there any stores you pass regularly, such as an ethnically focused food store, that you've never been into? If you venture inside, you might be pleasantly surprised by what's available, and they are bound to welcome your custom.

HOST AN ASYLUM SEEKER

For those fortunate enough to have a spare room, offering a safe, welcoming place to stay for a refugee child, family, or individual who would otherwise be sleeping on the street is an incredible way to reach out to somebody with vastly different life experience. Not only does it protect them from exploitation and worsening health, but it gives them a secure base from which to engage with solicitors. The whole family will learn from hearing about their values and customs and discovering common ground.

START SOMETHING

If there's little in your area for you or your child to join in with, you could be the person to start something. Whatever your passion, reach out on Nextdoor, Facebook, or whichever local forum gets most traffic, and invite others to join you in singing, dancing, playing a sport, chatting in Japanese, or crafting.

GET INVOLVED

Instead of steering clear of school events (if you do), consider helping out at a summer fair or quiz night, or lend your services to the teachers taking pupils on a class outing, or come into school as a reading volunteer. Help is usually gratefully received, and it's an opportunity to meet some of the other children and families your child mixes with every day who aren't their special friends.

BUILD A COMMUNITY

Help your child recognize, celebrate, and play their part in local, national, and global communities. Their actions and choices can shape and change the world.

FAMILY TIES

Whether there are two of you or 10 of you, your family is your most precious community. Create a loving, resilient, and outward-looking unit.

Asupportive home environment is the biggest advantage you can offer your child as they grow up. Knowing who they are, what's expected of them, and that they are loved will give them security and confidence, ready to explore the world and cope with setbacks as their independence increases. Learning about their family roots can also give them a deeper sense of where they come from and how they fit and connect with the rest of the world.

LOVING HOME

A supportive family community is one whose members show they care, communicate with each other, and behave in predictable ways. Create a warm, loving environment by rewarding positive behavior with your attention. Thank your child for any kind or helpful words or acts, however small, and properly engage with them, with smiles and eye contact, on a regular basis as you chat or do a game or activity together. Accept that active negotiation and compromise will always be necessary in family life. By teaching your child how to care for others at home, you make it more likely that they will take these behaviors out into the world.

In a strong family community, children know what to expect each day and know their own part in making life run smoothly. A family routine—from pizza on a Monday night to sorting the laundry together on a Saturday morning—will make life easier to manage for everyone. Build times into your week where you will be able to talk to each other properly. Allowing all members of the family regular opportunities to express how they are feeling will help prevent anger and frustration from building up. You don't need to solve everyone's problems, just be ready to hear them. Remember to look after your own needs—diet, exercise, hobbies, and relationships—as well.

A strong family also has bonds with others outside the immediate unit. These might be close friends or extended family. It's worth nurturing relationships with those you trust who wish to be involved in your child's life. Visits, phone calls, and video calls will help establish and maintain a connection. Over the years, your child may build up independent relationships with these special people, giving you and them someone else to turn to for additional help and support when needed, as well as fun times.

DETECTIVES

Have you always lived where you are now, or did you move there recently?

What about your grandparents or parents—do they live round the corner or on the other side of the country or world? Creating a simple family tree that traces where as well as when your ancestors lived can be a fun and eye-opening project for your child—and perhaps you, too. You can create a family tree online or download a template to fill in or draw your own, adding photographs of relatives and sketches (or photo collages) of how, from your research, you imagine your ancestors looked. Researching the meaning of your family name can also be revealing.

See how far back (if at all) you have to go to find relatives and ancestors living in a different country or speaking a different language. Most written records of births, marriages, and deaths go back only three or four generations, but this doesn't have to be an onerous research project. Your child might enjoy interviewing family members—in person or online—about what they can remember about their own grandparents or even great grandparents. Some children might be inspired to investigate their ancestors' birthplaces—or just agog to discover how far around the world their family tree extends.

FARIBA SOETAN

LIVING ROOTS

My belief in teaching children about their roots stems from my own upbringing and lack of understanding about where I came from. I was very young when we left Iran, and I often wonder what my parents could have done differently to teach me and my siblings about the immigration story that led us to a town in Alberta, Canada. Perhaps if we had known more about my Iranian grandmother, the language gap would have seemed less significant and I would have had more empathy when she came to stay. Settling in a small town after fleeing Iran following the Iranian Revolution, without any acknowledgment from my parents of the journey we'd made, meant I often felt out of place, searching for answers about who we were and where we came from.

Because of this, my partner and I believe in the importance of teaching our children their story. We've come to value the role that their grandparents play in this. My partner's family hails from a city in southwestern Nigeria called Abeokuta, which translates as "hide behind a rock." The history of his distant ancestors is a fun story for my daughters to hear over and over again—how they were able to resist their enemies for a time because the villagers were able to hide behind the rock. Though they live far away, their grandparents always have time to answer questions, even scheduling lessons in Yoruba (their local language) via Zoom.

It's been fulfilling to witness the girls grow into knowing and feeling proud of their heritage. When they were small, they understood their mixed heritage in the context of their different skin colors. Now, when they hear someone at school talk about Nigeria or they see it on television, they understand that there are people, histories, stories, and legends that come with being able to claim this identity. They also understand that they share this history with others, whether that's family, sports stars, or even celebrities. There's a pride that comes from a shared background.

On my side of the family, our daughters have been curious to learn about the cultural dress that their great grandfather would have worn and his lifestyle as part of a nomadic ethnic group in southern Iran. Geography class in school gives them even more context as they begin to understand that they share ancestry with someone whose lifestyle, religion, and well-being differed so fundamentally from who they are today. It's been no less fascinating for them to realize how their nomadic roots might have impacted generations since then—including their own mom—my journey took me from Iran, to Birmingham, England, then to Canada, and finally to London, which they call home.

"Our daughters' faces light up when they chat with grandparents and learn about their Nigerian ancestry."

These stories have brought their family tree to life, increasing their self-awareness and pride as they understand who they are and the journeys that led them here.

ACTION PLAN
Create a Bond

Families come in all shapes and sizes, and each variety has its joys and challenges. Find ways to strengthen family bonds, so your child has a secure base from which to explore the world.

BE INTENTIONAL

A positive family culture, where children and adults share values and work toward the same goals, is most likely to come about if parents actively consider and discuss what's important to them about family life and work to foster that. If your family had a mission statement or a motto, what would it be?

PLAN TOGETHER

Whether it's a family vacation or just what the menu plan is for the week ahead, involve your child in family decision-making wherever you can. This will give them a sense of control over the events in their life and make them feel like a valued part of the family unit.

SUNDAY SUPPER

If your days are hectic and it's hard to make time for family members you don't live with, find a regular slot to see, call, or chat with them online. This way they become part of the fabric of your regular household life, keeping up to date on the little things, not just the big news events.

PERSONALITY TREE

If your child has a particular hobby, temperament, or taste, they might like to create a family tree, not of dates and locations but of personalities. From their relatives and ancestors, who plays soccer, who is into fashion, who likes gymnastics? Does somebody else love liquorice and hate pickled onions? They might be surprised when their research shows they share their passions and predilections with other family members, near and far!

FAMILY HISTORY

Stories of how you and other family members have overcome ups and downs over the years, and come through trials together, can inspire and reassure children. Share information from your past, including special and scary moments in your family history.

NEW TRADITIONS

Perhaps you have your own family traditions from when you were a child that you'd like to continue now that you're a parent; or this might be an opportunity to create some brand-new ones special to you. From going to the same campsite every August to watching a movie in pajamas on Christmas Eve, making shared memories with loved ones will create strong family bonds.

LIVE LOCAL

Your household is just one in a network of many. Reaching out to your neighbors, and supporting their livelihoods, brings benefits for you and for them.

What makes your neighborhood a good place to live? Is it a thriving, bustling place or somewhere you tolerate because you grew up there? The arrival of a new baby makes your physical world shrink, and your local neighborhood takes on a new importance, both for friendships and facilities. While your horizons expand as your child grows, family life continues to revolve around your local community.

HELP OUT

When children are familiar with people and places, it makes them feel safe. A friendly wave to neighbors out and about and a smile and hello each time you see the school lunch person, the mail carrier, or anyone else you come into regular contact with will make them feel grounded and secure. Making full use of the playgrounds and facilities near home will allow you to build up connections as you run into the same people and start to recognize faces and names.

Help your child become aware that they are part of a street or village community. If there are any frail or lonely people on your street, they might be delighted to get to know your family and enjoy the sight and sound of children playing. You might keep an eye out for nearby elderly residents and even offer them your number for emergencies. Being gracious about taking in a package for your neighbors or putting their garbage out when they're away will hopefully mean they return the favor. As well as helping them, a good local network will be invaluable if ever your teenager locks themselves out or wants to start earning some pocket money by babysitting.

You might prefer to get involved in your local community in a more structured way, by joining a group or volunteering. There may be a local food bank that welcomes help. A community fridge is a registered place where local businesses and individuals can donate surplus food (from a community garden, for example), which those in need can collect for free. From sports, music, and arts clubs to organizations that give back to the community, such as Scouts, Cubs, and Brownies, there are also bound to be groups your child could get involved with.

SHOP AROUND

The more locally grown your family's food is, the fresher it will be, and the more environmentally friendly, too, as it won't have traveled hundreds of miles to reach you. Is there a local food stand or a produce box subscription that you can sign up to? Perhaps a weekly excursion to a farmers' market could become part of your family routine. Or maybe your local baker delivers bread that they've made themselves that morning.

As well as shopping locally for food where possible, support the other stores and your neighborhood restaurants, cafés, bars, theaters, pubs, and music venues. When you shop near home, whether in person or online, you pump money into the local economy, saving and creating jobs as the business owner in turn employs local tradespeople and suppliers.

Shopping locally isn't a purely altruistic act. Often local business owners are adept at meeting the specific needs of their community and can be more flexible than the large chains about letting you "try before you buy." They will also often support local charities, such as school fundraisers, donating raffle prizes, for example. They tend to be entrepreneurial, with bookstores, cafés, and craft stores running inspired events. Their innovation and creativity, bolstered by your participation, can help build a local community that your family is happy to engage with, where you all feel safe and supported.

JEN PANARO

STYLISH SOLUTIONS

For as long as I can remember, I've felt "meh" about my hair. It's straight, simple, and pretty low maintenance, but it always felt boring and flat. I spent years getting expensive haircuts I didn't love. Occasionally, I'd bring photos of celebrities from magazines and ask the stylist to match the "look." But really?! It likely took a team of stylists hours to achieve the celebrity's red carpet 'do. I couldn't replicate that.

Then I stumbled on a great trick to find a local perfect stylist. Searching on social media using #hairstylist and the name of my town, I found a stylist I loved and who shared photos of her styles on other clients with hair like mine. When I landed in her chair for my first appointment, I showed her images of my desired style from her own social media account. She knocked it out of the park! Thanks to that quick online search, I've had the same hairstylist for four years, and she's right in my local community, working for an independent, eco-friendly salon.

While social media has its flaws, it is a great way to find local artisans and experts. Through hashtags and explore functions, I've discovered amazing local companies, including a vintage ice-cream truck that visits birthday parties, a science teacher who offers weekly sustainable science experiments for kids, and a local game company that sells the best-ever board games for our family games nights.

> **"Supporting small businesses helps create a strong local economy and makes our communities thrive."**

While it might appear silly to gush about social media helping me find the perfect hairstylist, the hack is so much more than hair. Consistently patronizing local services can transform communities into thriving economic districts, and social media can help us find those amazing businesses to bolster.

ACTION PLAN
Be a Good Neighbor

Set a good example for your child and together help make your neighborhood a great place to grow up. Small acts of kindness and a little effort can make a big difference to your community.

SHOUT ABOUT IT

If you've used a local service or bought something from a local store and you've had a good experience, let the world know. Recommend them to friends, and if the business is plugged in to social media or has a website, write a review for them, or like or share their posts.

KEEP AN EYE OUT

When you see families who live in your street or near by, smile and say hello. Recognizing children means you can keep an eye out for them as they're out and about—say, walking home from school—so you can be an active bystander if necessary, making your neighborhood safer.

IN YOUR CART

Many supermarkets have a collection point near the checkout for donations for a local food bank. Slipping just one extra item in your cart that your child can then add to the donation box can make the world of difference to a local family.

GO PLOGGING

From the Swedish words "jogga" (jog) and "plocka upp" (pick up) comes a new verb: plogging— picking up litter when you're out jogging. It's a great activity to do with your child and is good exercise, as it adds squatting, bending, and stretching to running (or walking!). Wear gloves and take a bag to collect the trash—see which of you can find the most. If you're feeling fired up, you could go one step further and organize a community cleanup.

LEND A HAND

If a neighbor is going on vacation, offer your family's help to water their garden, feed their cat, or take care of their hamster while they are away. Your younger child can do this together with you, or your teenager might be able to take on some tasks independently.

STOCK UP

Sometimes shopping locally can feel less convenient than ordering from a big retailer online. Thinking ahead can help make it viable; for example, stock up on birthday cards or presents for the next couple of months when you go to a local craft market, especially if there are discounts for buying several items. You could make a trip to local independent shops or market stalls a weekend family outing.

THINK
GLOBAL

Every time you decide which brand of
chocolate to buy or add bananas to
your shopping basket, you are affecting
somebody else's livelihood in the global
supply chain.

Even in developed countries, we are dependent on raw materials and manufacturing from elsewhere in the world to maintain our standard of living. By importing goods, we support farmers and producers all over the globe, provided we pay a fair price for the riches that other regions, including developing countries, have to offer. The way a click of the mouse can cause a package to appear at your front door a few hours later can seem magical, even to adults. Children certainly lack the depth of understanding to appreciate all the work of harvesting, manufacturing, and fulfillment that goes into stocking the supermarket shelves, but the human effort behind these endeavors is huge and needs to be rewarded appropriately.

SUPPLY CHAIN

When you buy a T-shirt from a chain store, it may well have been made in Dhaka, Bangladesh, using cotton grown in India, China, or the US. Your smartphone started its life as raw materials that had to be extracted from the Earth, perhaps in China, and then transformed into the phone's components before being assembled in a factory. Apple procures components from more than 200 suppliers for their devices. Most of the

five billion bananas we buy from supermarkets each year have been grown in Latin America, thousands of miles away. The bananas take around nine months to grow and then must be harvested, washed, sorted, packaged, and transported to the container ships that will carry them far away. As Martin Luther King Jr. said: "Before you finish eating breakfast this morning, you've depended on more than half the world."

Just because something is sold by a US retailer, therefore, doesn't mean that the workers in the supply chain have had access to the same rights, wage, and safeguards to their health and safety that a US worker would expect. Big companies may have links with workers all over the globe— miners, factory workers, farmers, fulfillment companies. The raw materials might be available only from a handful of specific locations, and a big company may choose to site its manufacturing wherever is most cost effective—for example, in low-cost economies, where wages are low.

FAST FASHION, CHEAP CHOCOLATE

Supermarkets will compete for the best deals for goods in order to win customers with the cheapest prices possible. The Fairtrade Foundation is a global movement that works to make trade fair for farmers and workers so that producers in developing countries—of cocoa, bananas, coffee, cotton, and more—are paid a wage that enables them to farm sustainably and enjoy a reasonable quality of life. By buying fairtrade produce in the stores, you are accepting the true cost of the items you purchase, which allows the producers' children to go to school and live in decent accommodations.

Some companies work directly with their suppliers, as employers, to ensure that they know who is doing what at every stage of the supply chain for the products that they sell. This way they can guarantee the workers are paid a living wage. Without this appropriate wage, children become victims of child labor, as parents need their labor to make ends meet. In Ghana and the Ivory Coast, where more than half of the world's cocoa is cultivated, hundreds of thousands of children are made to work long hours using sharp tools and carrying heavy loads. Some are even forced to work outside the family by farmers who can't afford to hire adult workers. Forced labor is the most common form of modern slavery, the severe exploitation of other people for personal or commercial gain. Of

the 40 million people estimated to be trapped in modern slavery worldwide, one in four of them is a child.

As a consumer, and part of the global community, you have the power to support the fairtrade producers and ethical companies by paying the extra penny or pennies it costs to safeguard workers' well-being, ensuring factory infrastructure and working methods meet essential health and safety standards and that there is a living wage for adults. You can choose to boycott the big companies that turn a blind eye or worse to the working conditions of the laborers in their supply chain. This includes not taking responsibility for the environmental impact of their business. By involving your child in your spending decisions, you open their eyes to the impact these have and normalize responsible purchasing.

The other way to support the global community of workers is to reduce demand for cheaply produced goods. Sending your child to school on Christmas sweater day in a sweater swapped with a friend, not one bought new, will give you a genuine glow when you remember you are contributing to another child in the global community being able to attend school at all that day.

JEN PANARO

FASHION FORWARD

When I was a teenager, I looked forward to shopping for a few new things for my closet each fall before school started. Back then, we headed to the mall to buy new clothes, and I never thought to shop secondhand. In the decades since, the landscape has changed dramatically. Fast fashion and textile waste have skyrocketed. Fortunately, the secondhand clothing market is transforming as well and looking to compete with traditional clothing retailers.

As our children pine for new outfits at the start of the season, consider encouraging them to purchase items secondhand. There are so many options for finding great, stylish clothes for kids and teens, from thrift (charity) shops, consignment stores, and online resale stores. Here are a few tips to help make secondhand shopping feel relevant and fresh:

• Make a special day of visiting secondhand stores. If a child feels like shopping secondhand is less exciting than a trip to the mall, make the day feel extra special. Grab lunch at a favorite café between stores, or enjoy a special dessert at the end of the day.

• Shop with a phone but no money. Visit the mall without your wallet. Let your fashionistas explore the mall and take photos of things they love to gather inspiration. Then head to consignment shops or online resale sites to look for similar items. Kids experience the energy of the mall and peruse the latest fashion trends without participating in the fast-fashion churn.

• Create a friendly catwalk competition. Challenge your kids and their friends to compete for the best new-to-them outfit. Mix and match pieces in the dressing room, or have a fashion show at home.

Our kids want to protect our Earth, and teens, in particular, realize their future depends on it.

> **"By shopping secondhand, kids are sure to find amazing clothes without feeding the fast-fashion frenzy."**

JAMES *MURRAY*

INFORMED CHOICES

On a shelf in our boys' bedroom is a toy that doubles as a historic artifact. It is a beautifully constructed wooden truck that originally belonged to a family friend. On the base is a sticker that reads "Made in West Germany."

Such toys no longer exist, and not just because it was made in a country that is no more. Wooden toys have been largely replaced by plastic, which are typically manufactured in Asia and shipped thousands of miles. Before a baby is even born, they boast a global footprint, with their parents' choices impacting everything from Indonesian rain forests to Chinese air quality.

I remember as a child being fascinated by the labels showing where products were made. T-shirts from Bangladesh, drinking glasses from France, toys from, well, West Germany apparently. Each label was a little window on the big wide world. Now, as an adult, it is possible to explore the complexity behind these labels. Knowing where something comes from prompts other questions: why was it made there? What impacts did it have? How did it get here?

In my day job writing about green businesses, we often attempt to answer these questions. As such, we frequently report on how corporations pledge to cut their greenhouse gas emissions, only to find the bulk of their carbon footprint originates in their supply chain. Even companies or products that seem to have relatively modest carbon footprints see their impact expand by orders of magnitude when the emissions from the ships, factories, and mines they rely on are accounted for.

From here, it is possible to construct an argument about all that's wrong with globalization, with multinationals cast as neo-colonial environmental vandals.

There is plenty of evidence to support this hypothesis. China is the world's largest polluter, but only because it manufactures much of the world's stuff. Between 2015 and 2020, the planet was still losing an estimated 24.7 million acres of forests a year. From cotton and textiles to minerals and electronics, child labor remains scandalously present in global supply chains.

But there is a counternarrative. According to the UN, the share of the world's working population living in extreme poverty halved during the 2010s; the infant mortality rate has almost halved this century; and the percentage of children completing primary school rose from 70 percent in 2000 to 84 percent in 2018. The world is far from perfect, but some things have gone right.

The fear is that as the climate crisis escalates, the economic system's ultimately unsustainable nature will throw progress into reverse. One of the challenges of the age is how to accelerate globalization's positive trends while fixing its myriad flaws. The message for children is that while political and business leaders have an outsized role to play in tackling systemic problems, we can all play our part.

Our consumption choices have consequences, but it is possible to minimize their impact by avoiding unnecessary purchases, opting for products that carry accreditation labels that require supply chain oversight, such as Fairtrade or Rainforest Alliance, and rewarding those businesses that proactively work to curb their impacts, monitor their suppliers, and treat their employees and partners fairly.

> *"Our consumer behavior has consequences, and we can play our part in determining what they are."*

Most of all, though, we can inform ourselves about the complexity of the system of which we are all a part. Buying local has benefits but is not a panacea, and all choices contain trade-offs. Palm oil, for example, is a driver of deforestation, but it is also a high yield crop, which, if replaced by alternative vegetable oils, could lead to other land-use impacts.

There are no easy fixes, but that does not mean we shouldn't try to make good choices. We can start by asking where our latest toy came from, because in 20 years it, too, could be evidence of a world transformed.

ACTION PLAN
Spend Wisely

Use your purchasing power to have a positive impact on the lives of global workers. Explain to your child which companies you buy from and why, and why you buy only items that you really need.

ETHICAL SHOPPING

Research your favorite brands and service providers to see how they score on protecting human rights and the environment. This includes banks and investment funds. Then switch brands if necessary and let the company know why. The Good Shopping Guide online is a useful place to start for information.

RENT IT

If your family likes to stay up to date with the latest technology, or you need something only for a special occasion, such as a projector for a family celebration, consider renting your tech, not buying it. This prevents broken or obsolete equipment from ending up in a landfill.

STAMP OF APPROVAL

Look for an accreditation logo on products. Key ones for food include the Fairtrade Foundation, the Soil Association, and the Vegetarian Society. The Forest Stewardship Council (FSC) provides independent verification of sustainable wood and paper products.

CONSUME LESS

There's peer pressure at school from a young age to have what other people have. Often the single classmate who is richer or has more looms larger in a child's eyes than the many who have far less. Make sure your child is more aware of what they have than what they lack, and of what makes them happy. Young children are particularly susceptible to advertising. Mute ads when they appear on TV or online so they don't worm their way into your child's brain.

CLEAN UP YOUR ACT

Toxic chemicals in cleaning products can be harmful for children's health as well as for the environment when they're washed away into our waterways. Choose eco-friendly cleaning products and explain the labels to your child so they understand your choices.

BRAND AWARE

Your child can become brand aware, too. If they love chocolate, encourage them to sample different products and make the companies that prioritize the well-being of their workers their new favorite suppliers. If cartoon-festooned packaging sways them more than altruism when it comes to juice or yogurt, try a blindfolded taste test to encourage them to switch to a more ethical choice—or, if necessary, save the packaging and decant.

HUMAN CONNECTION

Trade, technology, migration, and our shared environment give humans many points of connection in the modern world. We can turn this interconnectedness into community.

From Neanderthals living in small, isolated populations to densely populated cities of millions, human society is now the most connected it's ever been. It can be as rewarding to foster meaningful bonds with someone at the opposite end of the country, or on a different continent, as it is to connect with like-minded people you meet in your local area.

CELEBRATE AND CONNECT

Deeply held passions and interests—whether cultural, spiritual, or humanitarian—can help you find your tribe and feel part of one of the rich communities that make up our global society. Enjoying sports, music, drama, or dance as a member of a crowd can feel richer than watching alone. Coming together with strangers for a common cause, as teenagers the world over did for the school climate strikes, can be thrilling and empowering. Charities such as Save the Children and Amnesty International can help us join forces with like-minded individuals. Faith-based celebrations or services of thanksgiving, such as Veterans Day, allow us to experience profound feelings as a collective, wherever we are from.

FARIBA SOETAN

EMOTIONAL TIMES

My children are aged five, seven, and nine years old and often turn to me when we're at a concert, in a church, or even simply watching a fireworks display among hundreds of others and ask, "Mom, are you crying again?!"

There is something incredibly emotional about being part of something bigger than just yourself, caught up in a feeling that touches crowds of people. It forces you to be 100 percent present in that moment. I don't apologize for it because I am aware of the power of connection and the impact it has on my well-being. For me, singing or listening to a choir during a church service is when I experience that connection most intensely.

The COVID-19 pandemic has taken its toll on many families throughout the world who have experienced despair and loneliness during lockdowns, unable to meet up with friends, family, and others in their familiar local settings. But the pandemic has also taught us that we can connect and have collective experiences in a different way, even though we're cut off from our usual local community.

To fill that important lockdown void, my family and I made an effort to join in with friends over Friday night disco parties, organized Netflix watch parties with extended family, and even took part in online scavenger hunts organized by the kids' teachers to help the children stay connected to their classmates and improve their mental well-being.

> **"I get goosebumps being part of the choir's collective voice during a church service, and it lifts me up."**

We missed our Sunday church services immensely and sometimes felt tempted to stay inside our bubble and not engage with the world, but emotional connection fuels my family to keep going—and I know how vital it is for us all.

DR MELERNIE MEHEUX

SOLIDARITY SPORTS

More than one in four children grow up in poverty—4.2 million in the UK in 2018–2019. Their struggle to have basic needs met, such as housing, food, and clothing, means they don't experience play opportunities the way other children do.

Being chair of the board of trustees of the charity Solidarity Sports is an honor and privilege. Based in West London, the charity was established in 2007 and supports disadvantaged children and families to overcome the effects of poverty, including limited recreational opportunities. More than 200 individual and corporate volunteers offer families wrap-around support, including chances to play, during school breaks and weekends. Over time, we have added mentoring programs, healthy eating initiatives, art activities, trips, and vacations in the UK and abroad to our remit.

In addition to difficult economic circumstances, many accessing the charity have experienced trauma. We work closely with social care and other agencies, supporting children in and on the edge of care, when their families are unable to meet their needs.

> *"Children and parents accessing the charity become part of a large family and are embraced and supported."*

Tragically, many of the families who access Solidarity Sports were affected by the Grenfell Tower Fire in 2017, where 72 people lost their lives, including some of our members. We aim to give families the opportunity to experience joy and create happy memories.

Solidarity Sports receives generous support, without which we could not operate. If you have time and resources, consider donating, volunteering, or encouraging your employer to contribute to a charity that can help children who are missing out; and if you or your child are struggling, know that there are charities to turn to. The embrace of our community can help us all endure difficult experiences.

ACTION PLAN
Be Passionate

Our shared experiences can transcend geography and nationality. Encourage your child to connect with others through their passions, from sports, music, and dance to faith or friendship.

FIND A FORUM

If your child has an unusual interest, social media can be a wonderful way to find people who share even the most eclectic of hobbies and to engage with them wherever they are in the world. It can also provide an outlet and support. You or your child may feel able to ask questions and confess to feelings online that you wouldn't discuss with friends.

LET CREATIVITY HAPPEN

Silence and solitude can be wellsprings for creativity, and time alone is important for children to find their own resources and draw on their imaginations. They don't need to be always connected—but sharing their creations once they are made can forge links with others.

BE MINDFUL

Older children in particular may find yoga or mindfulness (for example, sitting calmly coloring in, using books aimed at adults or teenagers) bring them a peaceful sense of being connected to something bigger than themselves. This can be very relaxing.

SEEK ENLIGHTENMENT

Children learn about different religions at school, but facts and figures aren't the same as truly understanding how faith—or a lack of it—permeates the culture and daily life of a friend whose family practice a religion or lifestyle you're not familiar with. Motivate your child to be curious about the beliefs and rituals of different people in your community, and gain insight as you find out more together, from books, TV shows, and conversations.

BE AN OLYMPIAN

The Olympics and Paralympics unite the world as elite sportsmen and women gather to compete at the highest level. Encourage your child's interest in watching or playing sports, from diving to trampolining, so they appreciate the sportsmanship and skill of athletes from all nations.

MAKE MUSIC

We can usually identify a lullaby, love song, or dance anthem from another culture even when we don't understand the lyrics. Music is a universal language that people on opposite sides of a political debate or with diverse backgrounds can share. It can also help us bond over an experience. Let making, listening, and dancing to music be part of your family life.

STRENGTH IN NUMBERS

We cannot survive in isolation.
Building a strong community takes
effort, but humans are uniquely
equipped to do this successfully.

Studies have shown that a person's social networks have a tangible impact on their physical health. Social support is particularly important in increasing resilience and promoting recovery from illness. Humans need strong communities—and have the capability to create them. We are distinct from other animals in the advanced ways in which we can collaborate with others. We successfully cooperate with people we hardly know, or strangers, to achieve far more than we could alone—from sending a person to the moon to developing a new vaccine.

COLLABORATION

Teamwork and cooperation are wonderful skills to teach children that will stand them in good stead for their working life as well as relationships near and far. Perhaps your child will build a taller tower if they work with someone else; cleanup time will certainly go faster if everyone chips in.

To function successfully, our societies need rules, laws, customs, and systems that are accepted as reasonable and fair by the majority. Balancing the needs, rights, and opportunities of individuals in a fair society is at the heart of social justice. You can teach your child to collaborate and to respect the rules at home and at school, talking them through where necessary and helping them understand how these are designed to help life run smoothly for everybody.

FAIR PLAY

Food and clean water, education, employment, health care, and physical security—in an ideal world everybody would be able to access these things, and all humans deserve them equally. When children are asked to share something, such as a cake, they usually have a profound sense of what's fair and are likely to display outrage if one child has so much as a crumb more than the others! It's easy for them to see how greed is detrimental to other people's well-being. You can also demonstrate that when there's a limited supply of something desirable—say, sweets—agreeing in advance on how you're going to divide them up, and on what basis, will make sharing less likely to end in tears. While it's simplistic, this can help your child understand the inequities of discrimination, and of rich nations profiting from poorer ones, and demonstrate how fairer allocation of resources can help keep the peace.

In large family gatherings, it's also often noticeable to children (and even more so to adults!) that the "government" of parents cannot always legislate for every issue, and the group will often devise its own modus operandi, with teenagers taking charge of younger children, for example. Civil society—voluntary and community organizations, and individuals who unite for a common purpose—has an important role to play in making life run well. Children can learn with siblings and friends how important trust is for relationships in strong communities, and how this is something that has to be earned over time.

Understanding the dynamics of the schoolroom, their family, and groups or clubs, even at a basic level, can help your child appreciate how communities operate. You may like to explore together charities that work with children, such as UNICEF (the United Nations International Children's Emergency Fund) so that they see how, for many children both at home and abroad, life is not fair—but we can work to change that.

We cannot survive alone. By investing and taking pride in your communities—both inside your home and around the globe—you show your child how to do the same.

DR MELERNIE MEHEUX

TEAM GOALS

Collaboration, mutual respect, problem solving, and shared views and beliefs are core values of a successful community, where everyone lives peacefully side by side. Belonging and cohesion are the fabric of society, and learning to successfully interact with others, even just a select few, is important for children's development. Working within teams develops listening and leadership skills as well as confidence, empathy, and compassion for others. These are all skills we want to nurture within our children as they learn to successfully navigate and shape the world.

Children develop understandings of teams from their own "tribes" at home. What children see and experience contributes to successful development of cooperation and team-building skills. Everyday activities and routines develop community skills in our children. At home, we can develop these at a basic level through family rules, rotas, and responsibilities, reinforcing the notion of collective responsibility. We can teach children to follow rules by linking jobs to rewards such as reward charts or Special Time—dedicated, planned family time together. Typically, children will be motivated when they have a say in choosing rewards!

Gardening and washing dishes can be supported tasks for young children or independent jobs for teens. It's important that children understand the value of keeping living spaces reasonably tidy, including bedrooms. Even very young children can help by sorting trash for recycling. From preschool to teen, every child can have a role, purpose, and function, creating a sense of belonging.

You can also work as a family unit to help others through your choices and actions. Encourage children to donate unwanted clothing and toys to charity, explaining why we recycle to help disadvantaged children and families. Shop with your child and buy ethically, explaining your choices—for example, how buying fairtrade contributes to social justice, ensuring that traders across the world, including some of the most vulnerable, are treated fairly and not discriminated against.

"Children acquire essential skills from teamwork, as they connect and work to achieve common goals."

The COVID-19 pandemic reignited a sense of community and teamwork across the world. We shared gardens with families who didn't own one and donated laptops to homeschooled disadvantaged children living in poverty. Neighbors checked in on the elderly and vulnerable to ensure they didn't go hungry. We were fully connected to our communities. As society readjusts, we need to make sure we maintain these positive behaviors, for our children's sakes.

We can start this immediately with family and friends. We don't need grand gestures; instead, let's maintain momentum through small things like checking in on friends and neighbors.

MARVYN HARRISON

FAIR SOCIETY

These days, younger generations are more informed than ever about socioeconomic and political challenges that impact their lives. That's why it's likely that our children will come to us with their worldviews from an earlier age than we did ourselves. What starts as curiosity in younger children slowly forms into beliefs as teens. So how can we help our children develop strong perspectives and become well versed in social justice?

Social justice, which is fairness manifested in society, includes housing, welfare, environmental change, mental well-being, race and gender relations, as well as the policies and institutional norms that are involved in change. Our children will be exposed to informal social justice-related language like "woke" and "lefty" and more formal terms like "egalitarian," "pro-human rights," and "equality." Even though you have your own worldviews, your children will inevitably develop their own at some stage.

While you may sometimes feel the desire to question or challenge your children's views, it's incredibly important to have an open discourse with them at all stages. Give them space to work through their own ideas and provide different points of view when needed.

> *"Children slowly form beliefs around social justice that stem from the values you share with them."*

So if you believe in the idea of being a global citizen, make sure your children are aware and compassionate about social justice and its various intersections. In order to better inform their view of the world, try to have deeper conversations with them and show an interest in their views, whether or not you agree with them.

In a nutshell, your goal should be to help your children develop views that are strongly educated, supported by a larger perspective, and rooted in their personal values.

THINK OF OTHERS NEAR AND FAR AS YOU LIVE LIFE TO THE FULL.

ACTION PLAN
Work as a Team

Help your child learn to work as part of a team, and understand the importance of doing their fair share, both at home and elsewhere.

JOINT EFFORT

Give siblings or friends a project to do together and watch them figure out team roles; step in only if necessary. This could be creating a fort in the living room; filming a movie on a phone, complete with costumes and props; or baking together, serving up the goodies and cleaning up afterward.

FAMILY ROTA

Draw up a rota to share chores among family members so that your child gets used to doing their fair share from a young age. Adapt the rota as they grow up so by the time they are a teenager they are helping vacuum and prepare meals.

FOLLOW THE LEADER

If your child isn't sporty, there are plenty of games that can be played in teams of two or more. Try a quiz, Pictionary, or an Escape Room–style board game, or children can enjoy Sardines or Follow the Leader, where they choose a leader and follow them mimicking every action.

YOU'RE RESPONSIBLE

As well as taking their share in the general chores, give your older child a specific responsibility in the household that is theirs alone. Ownership of a task that serves the common goal of a smooth-running household builds trust and independence and is more rewarding than being nagged intermittently to do something. They could be in charge of watering the plants in a particular room or keeping tech items clean or putting away the weekly groceries.

TEAM SPORTS

Conventional team sports such as soccer or hockey are great for learning to work as a team—and so is a game of badminton, tennis, or table tennis in the park or a makeshift volleyball match on the beach!

BE BRAVE

Working as a team doesn't mean following the crowd. Talk to your child about collective responsibility—individual members of a group being accountable for the actions and decisions of the group as a whole. Explain too that small actions by a group can have a big impact on other people. If the group's choices will damage the environment or hurt another living being, your child needs to be brave and make their objections known.

SPEAK OUT

Help your child learn to think critically, develop an argument, and voice their opinion clearly and responsibly as they challenge the status quo for a better society.

LOOK AT THE EVIDENCE

Children naturally desire to do things differently from their parents' generation. To bring about positive change, they need to be able to make informed choices.

It's easy to mistake opinion for knowledge, for adults as well as children. We all see the world from our own unique perspective, the result of our upbringing, our cultural beliefs and values, and our lived experiences. Our daily routines can embed our habits and ideas so we forget that alternative approaches and outlooks are available. Technology can exacerbate this—for example, cookies on websites help ensure we see only articles and ads that corroborate our interests and beliefs, instead of showing us the true range of what the world has to offer. Often we need to make a conscious effort to be alive to divergent opinions.

POINT OF VIEW

Self-awareness—the understanding that your values and assumptions play a part in your beliefs—can be particularly hard for children to achieve, as they have limited experience of the world. Some values and assumptions are so deeply ingrained, even in us as parents, that it can be hard to realize they are interpretations, not facts.

A child can start to gain self-awareness by tuning in to their emotions and understanding the effect these have on their actions.

What makes them feel angry? Which activities spark joy? Draw attention to these moments in a light-touch way. When Grandma called to ask how the school assembly went, did they feel cared for? When their sister received amazing toys for her birthday, did they feel jealous?

Looking at picture books together can be helpful. Naming emotions is the first step to acknowledging them in order to then find ways to manage them successfully. Did they hit their sister when they felt jealous, or were they able to walk away from the taunting pile of toys or verbalize that they wished they had exciting gifts, too?

As children grow, you can help them understand that people see the world from different perspectives. A book a teenager remembers from elementary school as dense, long, and complex may suddenly look infantile, with its short chapters and big type. When different families go camping together, the children who arrive from the countryside may discover their city friends are disturbed by the open fields and rowdy birds. When messaging or chatting with friends, a jokey comment intended to be harmless might unexpectedly cause offense on a day when the recipient is feeling vulnerable or down.

ASSESS AND INTERROGATE

Children from a very young age have independent access to a range of information and entertainment that would have been unimaginable even 15 years ago. A great challenge for parents is how to encourage their child to be curious and independent-minded while keeping them safe. Although with younger children it is possible to control access to devices and content, once preteens and teenagers have their own phones and are socializing independently, it's more difficult and potentially counterproductive to police their viewing. So it's vital that children learn to assess and interrogate what they hear and see, rather than just accept it.

As a parent, you don't have to know all the answers. By exploring and investigating together whether a video or website is credible or trustworthy, you teach your child that we never stop learning and no one knows everything. Practice critical thinking together. Any claim you read should prompt a question, which will prompt another question. Where did this claim come from, and what is the evidence? You can help your child unpick their own assertions, such as "Everybody else is watching this movie." Who told them that—a lot of people or just one person? How reliable is that person and what led them to make this claim? Who is everybody—everybody in the world, country, town, school, class—or just everybody who happened to be at their cafeteria table at lunchtime?

INFORMED CHOICES

From toddlerhood onward, you can get your child into the habit of making informed choices. It's cold outside, so they need to add a layer before you walk to the park—do they choose their hoodie or their coat?

Of course, they may resist both, as they are warm at home and lack the experience to imagine feeling differently from how they feel in the moment. This is where your guidance is invaluable. However, recognize that your own assumptions are being challenged (and how uncomfortable that can be). Given how much more active they are than you, they may not feel the cold even once outside. If there's no frost, ice, wind, rain, or snow to put them at risk of hypothermia, do they definitely need another layer?

DR MELERNIE *MEHEUX*

REASONABLE
QUESTIONS

The development of moral reasoning—the ability to reason and judge right or wrong—is an important part of children's development. Recent psychological research says moral development is shaped by relationships, social environment, and the key adults in children's lives. This means parents, extended family, and teachers all have pivotal roles in developing children's critical thinking skills and their ability to challenge injustice and express opinions.

When children have new or radical ideas, it can be worrying for adults, particularly if their ideas don't fit with our worldviews. Many of us grew up not challenging or questioning information presented to us; however, some views we were taught to just accept we later found that they infringe the human rights of individuals in our society. Therefore, we must put fears aside and develop children's ability to evaluate information presented to them, whether on television, the internet, or during conversations. We need to give children confidence to voice opinions to friends at school and at home.

When young people are exploring new ideas, we can listen, ask curious questions, and ask for evidence to support their thinking. We can't assume a child is in the wrong. It might help to reflect on the positive activism of young people like the Fridays for Future climate action campaigners.

> **"Consider how different the world would be if Greta Thunberg's parents had censored her views."**

Society is catching up, and the voice of the child is now promoted. Behaviors such as assertiveness, self-direction, and passion challenge parents in developmental phases like the "terrible twos" and "argumentative teens," but these could be reframed as prerequisites for strong leadership in later life.

JESS PURCELL

CRITICAL EXPERIMENT

One of my long-term goals as a parent is to teach my children to think critically. As a former science teacher, it makes sense for me to use the wonders of the natural world as my platform to foster these skills. Science teaches us to ask big questions, like "how?" and "why?" and provides us with an organized pathway to either discover an answer to a question or lead us to a new one.

You can use the language of science far beyond the classroom to build confident, independent thinkers. And you don't need a science background to do it!

SCIENCE IN PRACTICE

Here's a simple activity that I did with my five- and eight-year-olds that can be used to build confidence in critical thinking.

After the first snowfall of the year, my children were curious about the time it would take for snow to melt indoors. So that's where we started. (Note: if you don't live in a snowy latitude, or it's not the winter season, you can substitute ice from the freezer for snow instead.)

First, we considered the factors (or "variables," in science-speak) that need to be taken into account prior to making a prediction. For our experiment, we discussed how indoor air temperature and the compactness of the snow could affect the time of melting, as well as the volume of snow that was collected. We chose to collect 2 cups (approximately 500 ml) of compact snow. This translates to real-world decision-making as gathering background information.

Once we'd discussed the variables that could affect our decision, we each made a prediction, also known as creating a hypothesis. I chose to reveal my prediction last, as I did not want my

> *"Science teaches us to ask the big questions and gives us an organized pathway to finding answers."*

thinking to influence my children's thought processes. We wrote them down on a piece of paper to make them "official."

Next, we gathered our supplies to test our predictions: 2 cups of compact snow brought in from outside and placed in a glass container on the kitchen counter. We recorded the time the snow was first brought in from outside, and then we waited. I was impressed at how many times my kids checked on the melting snow, noting the time that had passed at each inspection.

Once the snow finally melted, we calculated the time the snow had taken to change to a liquid state, then compared the answer to our hypotheses.

Then we made connections. How would the rate of melting change if the indoor air temperature was 1 degree warmer? Three degrees warmer? Two degrees cooler? How does this relate to the rate of melting snow outside? Further, how does the rate of snowmelt affect the local stream levels? What will happen to the rate of snowmelt at the North and South Poles when the average global temperature rises another degree? It's amazing how one simple question can turn into

a dozen more! You might tell them about the Intergovernmental Panel on Climate Change's finding that the average global temperature has already risen 1 degree Celsius and is predicted to continue to rise if world carbon emissions are not significantly reduced.

Making the connection between a simple experiment and the factors at play in our changing world can bolster your children's confidence in sharing their thoughts on actions to address local and global issues. No matter what you choose to explore, stick to these key points:

• Pick a question. Keep it simple.
• Do some background research on the topic.
• Make predictions.
• Test your predictions.
• Look at your results and make connections.
• And most important, investigate with your kids. Show them that learning never stops.

Building confidence in your children to be able to solve problems logically and think critically is crucial to their success in differentiating between fact and fiction. In an age of constant information, this is a vital skill.

ACTION PLAN
Think Critically

Encourage your child to be curious about the information they see and hear, and teach them ways to test its accuracy and purpose rather than automatically accept it.

TRUE, FALSE, FAIR

A simple question your younger child can ask themselves when they read or hear something is, is this information true or false, fair or unfair? How do they know?

SPOT GREENWASH

Greenwashing is when companies inflate their eco-credentials to increase sales. Some accreditations, such as "B Corp," are robust, whereas others, such as "free range," have a variety of meanings, from access to plentiful outdoor space for the animals in question to very little. Alert older children to marketing techniques.

DRAW UP A LIST

Figure out with your child which websites you both think are useful and reliable sources of information, whether for school or entertainment. With older children, this can prompt an interesting discussion over the integrity and approach of sites such as Wikipedia.

EVERYDAY SCIENCE

Science teaches children it's best to gather facts where possible, not guess. Here's how to test air quality inside and outside your home. Cut out two 2-inch (7 cm) squares of white cardboard, poke a hole in each, and thread some yarn through to make a hanging loop. Spread petroleum jelly on one side of each square. Hang one outside, and one inside. After a week, see what has collected. The fewer particles there are around you, the easier it is for your lungs to use the air.

ENCOURAGE QUESTIONS

Curiosity is a vital skill that will prompt your child to unpick assertions. Instead of shutting down your child's questions with vague responses, encourage them to research the answers and show them how they can do this safely online or through books or friends.

SHIFT OPINION

Demonstrate that changing your mind can be a good thing when it's in response to new information or a fresh perspective. Model reflective thinking: taking time to consider all angles. Sometimes it can take a generation for information and understanding to fully percolate; you can explain that certain attitudes, for example, around homosexuality, were often different in the past. What will we look back on with astonishment in years to come?

FIND THE RIGHT WORDS

Effective communication is our most powerful tool. Give your child the confidence and the words to be able to express their opinions and take on the views of others.

Thanks to social media, anybody can have a platform. School and the workplace also require us to speak out if we want our views heard. As well as encouraging children to question what they read and hear, we need to teach them the skills to communicate well themselves, both in person and online.

CONFIDENT COMMUNICATION

Your child's passions may be roused by learning that the orangutan is on the brink of extinction or that air pollution is now recognized as a cause of death. Help them harness these powerful emotions and find their voice in a constructive and effective way.

When their requests are regularly responded to, a child feels secure enough to display emotions and confident enough to ask for what they need. Even a newborn baby is in dialogue with his or her mother, who learns to interpret different cries—which usually sound identical to a stranger—as different messages: hunger, physical discomfort, tiredness. As the baby grows, boredom and frustration get added into the mix and can be particularly intense before a child learns to talk or walk.

Communicating through signing can help relieve the frustration of a baby who doesn't have words to convey their needs.

As your baby grows into a child, you can help them become a confident communicator by giving them airtime and not talking over them, even when they are slow to make their point and you think you know what they are going to say. Wait until they've finished before you respond. Listen with your whole body, and don't have one eye on the phone or TV. With a little one, you may need to kneel down so your faces are level. Allow them to take full part in family conversations so that they don't feel frustrated and have to shout to be heard.

Don't forget to share information yourself, too. Why should your child tell you about their day if you never reveal anything about yours? Your anecdote about a tricky colleague or a lunchtime encounter might trigger them to remember something that happened to them, too, and inspire them to talk it through or just enjoy recounting it to you.

To build your child's confidence, perhaps they can practice using their words to persuade you into something, such as additional screen time in return for chores. Let them in on the

secret that thinking about what the other person wants from the negotiation is vital to a good outcome. Winning an argument by arguing their case through will show your child the power words have to change lives! Each small success will boost their belief in their own ability to communicate, advocate, and persuade.

USEFUL PHRASES

Each new word a toddler learns, from "Mom," "more," and "no" onward, transforms their ability to convey their needs. Include useful words and phrases in your regular conversations with your child, that they can start to copy to make their communication more sophisticated. "That was kind" is a useful way to acknowledge that someone's efforts are appreciated. "I'm feeling angry because someone broke my favorite mug" can explain why the atmosphere has thickened and show that it's okay to admit to strong feelings. A simple "What do you think about that?" lets someone know that their opinion and contribution to a conversation is valued. "Why?" is a very powerful word that draws out others' views. "I don't understand" is also a phrase that can save a lot of time and upset. When your child is with other children, certain words will make playtime run more smoothly, such as "I'd like a turn now." If they need to be more assertive, they can say, "I don't like this," or "Don't do that," or "That's not okay." A simple, assertive "no" is powerful when necessary, as is the statement, "We don't do that here." "Please" and "thank you" oil the wheels of conversation generally, as does the word "sorry" when an apology is necessary. A proper apology expresses real remorse, takes ownership of the wrongdoing, validates the other person's feelings, and asks for forgiveness, smoothing the way for better future relations. "I'm sorry you feel that way" is not an apology since it doesn't admit to any wrongdoing on the speaker's part; it does, however, acknowledge that you have hurt the other person.

When communicating online, words can be easily misinterpreted. A simple starting point is for your child to ask themselves before they press Send how they would feel if they received that message and how would a parent or teacher react if they read the words? Teach them never to post a message they wouldn't feel comfortable delivering in person.

DR MELERNIE *MEHEUX*

FINDING A NARRATIVE

Psychologists say truth is socially constructed. What we believe to be right or wrong, true or false is dependent on how we see the world. This means it's essential for caregivers to model appropriate listening, narratives, and thinking.

With younger children, parents can comment on the world around them, asking questions about what they see to develop appropriate vocabulary. As children get older, we can begin to talk openly about real-life topics, such as environmental and world news, and model being aware of surroundings, having conversations about local communities. Teens will start to talk to family and friends about a range of issues, asking questions and exploring alternative narratives. Encourage questions, and prompt them to expand their answers, considering alternative solutions. You could ask: do you think that was the right thing to do? What could you do differently?

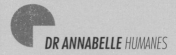

DR ANNABELLE HUMANES

TALKING THEIR LANGUAGE

My mother loves to tell the story of our camping trips to Ireland and Scotland. As a monolingual French speaker, I, apparently, used to spend hours hanging around other people's tents in the hope that I could strike up a conversation with someone. The fact that I was only three or four years old and spoke only French was never an issue. I would talk complete gibberish and try to imitate sounds of other languages to get people to understand me. While this is maybe not the most efficient technique, it usually worked. People would find it adorable and engage in the most fun conversations you can imagine about their family or their trip. I would find playmates almost every time that way.

Expressing yourself as a child can be done in many different ways—the most obvious being language. When you are growing up in a global community, you quickly realize that language can become a barrier. It does not have to be this way, though. Expressing yourself and getting your message across can be done despite a linguistic divide.

Finding the right words will be easier for our children if we expose them to different languages. When children understand that other people speak in a different way, and when they hear other languages often, it is a first step in overcoming communication barriers and learning to express themselves. It can also help to normalize difference and prevent prejudice.

> *"A smile is universal and breaks down all the language barriers in the world."*

There is no such thing as a universal language. Yet there are some words that are almost universally recognized. Iconic words and onomatopoeic ones like "boom!" or "sshhh!" can be understood in context, especially as they usually come with a gesture. There are also words that have spread through globalization—for example, "okay" or "ciao," or even "taxi" or "coffee," which sound similar in many languages.

It is no surprise that scientists have found that, when placed in situations where they have to convey a message to someone who speaks a different language, children will rely on gestures and on more or less elaborate charades. We can teach our children to express themselves using nonverbal communication. Baby sign language (not to be confused with American Sign Language or British Sign Language) is one tool that can be used with very young children to help them express themselves early on. In particular, if your child is immersed in a multilingual community, having a few basic signs that are common across the different languages has been shown to relieve frustration and facilitate communication with those closest. It can be useful to share with caregivers a few signs that your baby might use for "milk" or "more." It is also not uncommon to find that children keep on using those signs alongside speech later in childhood.

Gestures are not just for babies. Most gestures are culturally specific. Making a circle with the thumb and index means "everything is okay" in much of the Western world. In Japan, it means "money." In Brazil, it is something very rude! The "V" gesture with the index and the middle finger means "victory" or "peace" in the US, or is a cute, inoffensive pose for Chinese people. In the UK, when done with the palm of the hand facing your own body, it is the very opposite.... Helping our children understand and respect different cultures with nonverbal communication will greatly facilitate communication.

Playing games is also a fabulous way for children to engage together despite a lack of common language. My young daughter realized very quickly that communicating with her older cousins was hard work as she didn't speak their language fluently. Her youngest cousin, however, was easier to be with. All he wanted to do was play runaround games with her, rather than chat and exchange experiences. In their laughter and excitement, language barriers were overcome in minutes.

MARVYN HARRISON

POWER OF SPEECH

Our greatest power as humans is our language. Unlike any other species, our words can help us define who we are as individuals, build relationships, and even create or destroy the most complex of situations.

Whether those words are "I have a dream" by Dr. Martin Luther King Jr., or Emmeline Pankhurst's "trust in God; she will provide," words have the power to change the world at scale. That's why we must consider the feelings, thoughts, and actions that our words can provoke.

Equipping your children with the language to stand up for themselves and what they believe in starts with showing them your own integrity; providing them with the right books and media for them to consume; and talking openly about how their words affect others. The three skills that I constantly try to develop in my children are (1) How to use your words to clearly communicate what you mean. (2) Knowing when to say those words to the person who needs to hear them. (3) Understanding the external consequences and internal impact of being silent.

Through these skills, I want my children to recognize that activism isn't always Extinction Rebellion–scale protesting. An example of this is how people everywhere came out for their neighborhoods during the COVID-19 pandemic. When we "clapped for carers," we created an environment for health care staff to be prioritized and honored as a profession. When our children made rainbow paintings for our front windows, it moved others and brought communities together.

> *"You can help create change in your neighborhood or school by simply showing support and being vocal."*

At the end of the day, you want your children to understand that these things matter, no matter how small, and that they have the power to make a change.

FIND YOUR VOICE AND TAKE POSITIVE ACTION.

ACTION PLAN
Communicate Well

Teaching your child to take turns, listen, reflect, use words well, and empathize will help them communicate better so they can share their views and passions constructively and effectively.

GUESS THE OBJECT

This is a game for three or more players. Cut a hand-sized hole in a cardboard box. Place an object inside the box. One child puts their hand into the hole—no peeking!— and describes what they can feel. The others have to guess the object. If they succeed, the person with the winning descriptive powers gets a point. Then it's the next person's turn.

MIRRORS

Ask your child to think of an emotion, such as shocked, and then make their facial expression display it. You mirror the expression back at them and guess the emotion. Then swap! As well as helping them name feelings, it tunes them in to nonverbal cues, including eye contact.

SIMON SAYS

Simon Says is a great family or party game for active listening. The leader gives instructions such as "sit down" or "stand up," which the players must obey only when these are prefaced by "Simon says"— otherwise, they're out of the game.

FORTUNATELY, UNFORTUNATELY

A fun game for long trips that teaches taking turns and encourages rich vocabulary is "Fortunately, Unfortunately." The first person starts a story with a sentence beginning "Fortunately." The next player picks up the story, starting their sentence with "Unfortunately." The third speaker continues with "Fortunately" again. And so it goes on, until the hero comes to a fortunate—or unfortunate—ending.

HAPPY HUNT

For a scavenger hunt with a difference, challenge your child to bring you (quickly): an object that's useful; something that makes them feel happy; something they can't live without; something that comforts them; something that smells good. It might be revealing for both of you!

PB&J SANDWICH

Tell your child you will make them a peanut butter and jelly or chocolate spread sandwich—provided they can instruct you precisely how to make it. They can write down or speak their instructions. Then make sure you follow them absolutely literally. Depending on how clear, accurate, and precise their language is, your child may or may not get the sandwich they're expecting!

DISCUSS AND DISAGREE

As all families know, conflict of interest is inevitable in a community, whether that's the global one or the home! Teach your child how to argue a case and listen respectfully.

Disagreement is powerful and valuable. It's how new ideas come to be adopted. We should not expect to always agree with each other; if we do, we are exposing ourselves to a very narrow set of experiences and viewpoints. By teaching your child to talk through issues and disagree well, rather than be scared of conflict, you are arming them to play a part in society and, over time, gain the skills they need to persuade and be persuaded by others.

CLIMATE OF RESPECT

Everyone has a right to be heard—and that includes children. As a parent, it can be hard to be responsible for young people who see the world differently and regularly disagree with you, especially as you love them and can't just shrug off their disappointment or dismissal of your opinions. Respect their viewpoint. They are growing up in a new age, living a different childhood from yours.

A climate of mutual respect allows everyone to both express opinions and to challenge them, in a considered and considerate way. Children seek endlessly to understand what the boundaries and conventions are. Take what they say on board. Their curiosity and independent-mindedness are what will help them innovate, inventing sorely needed new solutions to difficult problems.

It can be helpful from a young age to establish ground rules for conversations in your household. For example: we take turns to speak; we speak calmly with no shouting or swearing (and save the discussion for later if we're too upset to have it right away); we don't always have to agree; we compromise; we take time to reflect on what the other person has said before coming to a conclusion. Often this can involve going away to research the facts—from whether eating cookies at bedtime really is bad for your teeth to how much screen time is reasonable and why. By involving children in the facts upon which you're basing your decisions, while they may still dislike the outcome, they are more likely to respect you for having a considered argument rather than just instinctively saying "no" to anything that bothers you. Debating facts rather than opinions also takes the heat out of the disagreement, preventing a clash of wills.

HEALTHY DEBATE

Children often love to argue back! Questions are a powerful tool for rooting out what people really believe and on what basis. Asking you lots of questions is a positive sign that your child is fully engaging with a topic and taking control of their own understanding. What's more, when they feel connected to an issue, and it feels personal, they are more likely to be motivated to enact change where necessary. As parents of toddlers and teenagers know, telling your child what to do rarely works. Let them come to their own decisions wherever possible, ensuring they have the facts.

Consider your own role when discussing an issue with your child. The default is usually for a parent to have a stated view, with the child arguing against it. Perhaps you could declare yourself neutral and ask your child to present both sides of the argument. Or you could play devil's advocate, encouraging them to argue against themselves. Teenagers might enjoy learning some debating basics, such as different types of arguments (for example, deductive and inductive), common logical fallacies (such as the false dilemma), and practiced techniques for winning over your opponent. If you're debating a highly charged issue, remember that no one can absorb a new idea instantly or change their stance right away. Allow time to reflect on the considerations a discussion brings to light, for you both.

JAMES MURRAY

BE TRUE

The legendary Hollywood producer William Goldman had a line about the movie business that makes for a sage observation in most fields: "Nobody knows anything."

Over the years, myriad books have been published with the dubious promise they can help you win friends and influence people. But for all the well-meaning advice on how to resolve conflict, conflict persists. It is an area where the Goldman doctrine applies.

The futility of the search for the perfect communications strategy has been particularly apparent in the fight against the climate crisis. For years, the fear was climate change was too big and scary a problem for people to grasp, so it was best to focus on the co-benefits that flow from decarbonization, such as green jobs and lower energy bills. Then along came Greta Thunberg who grabbed headlines by simply demanding leaders "tell the truth" about the true scale of the threat. Suddenly, campaigners started talking again in moral terms about the need to avert a climate emergency. But that in turn triggered a backlash and warnings that preaching by "elite" commentators would alienate people for whom climate change was not a priority. Better to focus on the co-benefits of climate action, some experts advised, taking the debate back to square one.

The truth is not so much that no one knows anything but that everyone is right. There are as many approaches to effective communication as there are people on the planet. Some are motivated by apocalyptic warnings, others by economic self-interest; some act on their responsibility as global citizens, and others prioritize threats to national security.

If there is no set playbook, there are broad principles that are useful for adults and children alike.

The first is to remember the simple truth that everyone is different. Everyone has their own interests, impulses, and inclinations. If you wish to resolve a conflict, you have to understand your opponents' concerns and priorities.

A degree of empathy enables the compromises that are essential for resolving any conflict. Children can grasp this reality early. What is the instruction to share, take turns, and think of others, if not a plea for compromise?

"Compromise is essential for resolving any conflict—but not at the expense of your integrity."

But, and this is important, when negotiating, it is vital to know your "red lines." Compromise is good; giving a free pass to racism, misogyny, violence, pollution, and injustice is not. There are times when conflict is unfortunate but necessary, when arguments have to be won, when bad faith actors have to be called out.

Whether in the playground or the negotiating room, conflict is an inevitable and painful part of life. When faced with conflict, it is crucial to be understanding, empathetic, and conciliatory. But you've also got to be true to yourself.

ACTION PLAN
Work It Out

Disagreement can be painful, but it's vital if we are to take new ideas on board and stand up for what we believe in. Help your child learn to argue well as part of a healthy relationship.

SWAP SIDES

If you and your child are having a friendly disagreement—say, about whether to do homework before or after dinner—once you've talked it through, swap sides and argue in the other direction. Finding all the pros and cons is great training in thinking of argument as a way to figure out solutions, not have a fight.

REWARD LOGIC

When your child comes to you with an argument as to why you should agree to something they want, if their reasoning is sound and their proposal is based on thought-through facts, reward that with agreement if you can.

AGREE ON SOMETHING

Teach your child that if they are struggling to resolve a dispute with a friend, it can help to find a point they both agree on, even if it's just that the sky is blue or ice cream is delicious! Managing to agree on one thing means they open the door to finding more to agree about.

MAKE A MAP

If your child is burning with emotion, there's no point attempting a rational conversation until they've calmed down. First, let them offload. Ask nonjudgmental questions to draw them out if necessary. Then, help them order their thoughts. Separate out the strands of their worries for them—perhaps there's embarrassment about something that's happened and anger about what might happen next. When the mess in their mind is tidier, together you can plot a route forward.

EXPLORE

Actively listen and explore your child's views, even if they shock or upset you. They might spot flaws in their own argument if you hear them out, and mastering your emotions is good role modeling. If they hold views you consider offensive, explain how these could hurt other people.

SET THE TONE

Often in an argument, people hear the other person's tone of voice more than they hear their words. Set the right tone for your conversation and your child is more likely to follow suit and adopt the same tone with you. Speak with respect for their opinion, display curiosity as to why they hold their views, and let them know you think they have an equal right to their position, even if you don't agree with it. This will help avoid a power struggle.

SHOW YOU CARE

From going on a march as a family to writing to your congressperson, bringing about change on a big scale requires active citizenship.

Every action we take has an impact on others in our community—and so does our inaction. Doing nothing about the issues we see people around the world struggling with is as much of a choice as doing something is.

There are many ways to be an active citizen, some more visible than others. Parents can help children learn how to engage in a responsible way, taking into account the law and ethical considerations and thinking through the consequences of their actions. Younger children will take their cue from you; older children will respond to wider influences.

RIGHTS AND RESPONSIBILITIES

Social movements, including Black Lives Matter, LGBTQ+ rights, women's rights, and many others, have brought burning issues such as racism and sexual discrimination to the attention of millions of people around the world, largely through their protest campaigns. Peaceful protest is a fundamental democratic right, with freedom of speech and the right to protest peacefully protected both by common law and by the Human Rights Act 1998. The police can impose conditions around the number of protesters and the duration of the protest—but only if they think this is necessary to prevent disorder or damage to property. By joining a march as a family, where appropriate and safe, as well as swelling the numbers, you show that the next generation cares, too.

Understanding how our democracy functions is fundamental to figuring out how to bring about change. Children aren't necessarily taught at school how the legal system works, nor the fact that access to legal services is not always equally available. Nor, often, do they learn about the role of the media, political parties, and trade unions. Parents can introduce these vital topics. Encourage your child to respect the rule of law, while realizing that the laws have been made by other humans and do not have to be set in stone. The law is there to keep us safe and enable us to resolve disputes without violence, giving the weak a voice as well as the strong. Everybody is equal under the law. However, laws need to be continually updated to reflect our changing world. Your child can influence who becomes a lawmaker once they are old enough to vote. Help them develop trust in our democratic and legal processes, while developing an understanding of the constraints and compromises inherent in democracy.

Sometimes campaigners feel that working within the law is ineffective, and movements use civil disobedience as a way to bring about changes. Whether an action is justified—such as missing school for climate strikes—is something to discuss openly with your older child. Help them work through the legal and ethical considerations, including the issues at stake, your family ethics, and the views of their teacher.

EVERYDAY ACTIVISM
Actions do not need to be grand or highly visible to make a difference, and children can play a powerful role in lobbying and shaking up the decision makers. A child can write to the chief executive of their local supermarket chain to protest about overuse of plastic packaging. They can write to their congressperson. They can set up a petition (probably with your help) and encourage people to sign it, or they can fundraise in imaginative ways to support a local, national, or global campaign run by a charity around an issue close to their heart.

Children can inspire the older generations to greater efforts because it is their future at stake. Local people might be galvanized into lending their support if they discover an environmental campaign isn't just about the rain forests and turtles on the other side of the world but also the litter-filled pond by the play area down the road. Your child can help them connect the dots. A hand-drawn poster displayed in the staff room or the town hall might have more impact than a professional ad. A school assembly run by the eco club might interest or affect the other pupils far more than a TV campaign would. It's true your child may need to be optimistic in the face of adult passivity and resilient in the face of setbacks—but your encouragement will support them.

A teenager may not want your involvement in their activism—rejection of the values of their parents' generation may be part of the point of their protest. Enabling teenagers to become independent is an essential part of parenting. If your child is saying something is a problem, is ready to show the world that they care, and is willing to take steps to fix it, then try not to undermine them by stepping in and taking over. You may need to talk through with them your desire to keep them safe and protected, and explain that your instinct is to help, as part of figuring out how you can be comfortable with them going it alone.

FARIBA SOETAN

LIFE LESSONS

One of the most powerful lessons I have ever taught my children was to take them with me to the voting station to elect our new MP—and help determine who the next prime minister would be.

It followed conversations we'd been having around the Black Lives Matter protests as my partner and I attempted to explain to our nine-, seven-, and five-year-old girls how their skin color could one day affect their opportunities. "But how is that fair?" we heard them ask, as I fought back the tears, determined to show we are NOT powerless and we don't need to be victims.

These conversations have since opened up further discussions about why, even with the best intentions, laws and rule makers can sometimes be unfair. My children will inevitably experience more of the injustices of our world (I can't control that), but my hope is that they take with them the message that they CAN make change happen.

MARVYN *HARRISON*

STAND UP FOR YOUR BELIEFS

"Daddy, why are the people so angry?" my son asked me during the summer 2020's protests for racial equality. At just five years old, my son was introduced to activism, which was triggered by the death of George Floyd and echoed by the words "Black Lives Matter." When I explained to him that a Black man had died unfairly at the hands of the police, it was that moment that I knew I was possibly ending my son's clear-cut understanding of good people (in his eyes, police officers) vs. bad people (i.e., criminals). But I knew it was my responsibility to show him how lines can be blurred and why speaking up against injustice is important.

After I told him this, he looked reflective and went quiet. While he didn't want to see the protest, we decided instead to make a BLM poster for our window—right next to the "clap for carers" rainbow we made a few weeks earlier.

That summer was my son's introduction to social justice and was even more significant because it involved a cause that directly impacted him, his parents, and his family. Becoming familiar with the Black Lives Matter movement allowed him to grasp just how many people were upset, and, of course, he wanted to support them.

> **"I am passionate about ensuring my children feel empowered to stand up for what they believe in."**

When it comes to the importance of racial equality and justice, I am passionate about ensuring my children are aware of these larger issues and able to stand up for what they believe in. And that counts for any part of their lives, from the unfair treatment of a peer at school to animal rights to local environmental issues.

The more your children know about topics that matter, and can be open with their opinions, the more they can become beacons of change just by showing they care.

JEN PANARO

VOTE WITH YOUR FEET

Growing up, my parents voted, but we never talked much about it, nor was I included in the process. When I turned 18 and was eligible to vote, it was a foreign process to me and not one with which I connected deeply. I didn't feel compelled to vote.

I recall the first time I walked into a voting booth, nearly a decade after I was eligible, and I wasn't sure what to do. While my parents did not intentionally bypass teaching me about voting, I wish I'd had more knowledge about the process as a kid. As parents, we can expose our children to the democratic process when they are young so they grow up expecting to be engaged voters and know why it's important.

We can include children in factual discussions of political platforms and agendas and show them how to research more about each candidate. We can watch political debates with them and reflect on the information shared.

Though kids cannot vote, caregivers can take them to the polls to observe the process or sit together to complete a mail-in ballot.

In our house now, we read books about voting and voting rights, including stories about people who didn't always have the right to vote and why this was important. We need our children to have confidence that voting is a powerful tool and that every vote matters. For my suggestions of books that support these lessons in democracy, turn to Resources (p.216).

> *"Exposing children to the democratic process when they are young helps them grow up to be engaged voters."*

To raise children who have the interest and ability to be activists in their community, they need to understand and be involved in the political systems that dictate how our communities operate. Parents are the first gateway to helping kids believe that their attention to the democratic process is meaningful.

ACTION PLAN
Do Something

Societal change for the better often comes from youth voices, and young people should be encouraged to believe in themselves and exercise their power responsibly. Little ones can help too, starting small.

CHALK ART

Whether it's a rainbow for health care workers or a heart to signify support for racial equality, pavement art can make a powerful and instant impact when it's adopted by a neighborhood, especially if the images are then shared via social media.

PROTEST

If you're going on a demonstration, make sure you talk it through with your child in advance, including the reasons why you are going, so that they know what to expect. Plan your route and print out a map with start and end points, and locate toilets. Write your cell phone number on your child's hand and agree on a place to meet if you get separated.

JOIN IN

There are a lot of active charities that welcome the involvement of young people. Here are a few: Action for Nature; Amnesty International; Roots & Shoots; UNICEF; Youth for Human Rights International; Youth for Our Planet.

FUNDRAISE

Encourage your child to turn sadness about a situation, such as homelessness or endangered animals, into fundraising action. They could suggest ideas to their teacher for school events—for example, a bake sale, sponsored silence, or class bike or car wash. Or you could try fundraising at home or in your street, perhaps with a garage sale, or even by organizing a Play Street day, where families whose children play outside make a donation.

TRAILBLAZERS

If your child feels passionate about a cause but doesn't know how to take action, help them research a role model in whose footsteps they can follow. They can find both inspiration and practical tips from someone who's stood up for what they believe in against the majority.

SAY IT'S A PROBLEM

Teach your child that showing you care can be as simple—and challenging—as one small, brave gesture. If a classmate is being unfairly treated, whether that's left out of a game or teased or pushed around, the act of speaking up for them when others are silent, or putting an arm around their shoulders, can be a powerful, life-changing act of courage.

PLAY TOGETHER

Technological advances put the world at our fingertips. Help your child have fun online in a safe and rewarding way, and enjoy stories and games together from a wide variety of countries and cultures.

OPEN MINDS

Our lives as global citizens today are rich beyond our ancestors' imaginings. We have all the resources we need to open our children's minds to the wider world.

In the 21st century, we can watch a video made by a stranger in their kitchen on the other side of the world or explore a website aimed at citizens of a different country. Alongside your family's favorite movies and books, try to incorporate fresh types of cultural experiences into your day-to-day living, giving your child a taste of the extraordinary variety of thought and stimulation that's available.

READ, WATCH, LISTEN

Reading books has always been a unique way to gain insight into other lives, and e-books make it easier than ever to access stories from authors based all over the globe. Use an e-reader or app to access a new world of e-books, which you can often borrow from libraries. Fiction can resonate profoundly with its reader and reveal new perspectives, helping a child feel empathy for an unfamiliar character confronted by unfamiliar experiences.

Movies, TV shows, online videos, podcasts, theater (live or streamed), and websites can also take you and your child on a journey to a different country, community—or universe. Why not listen to a different radio station one morning—perhaps a local show or a world service via the internet?

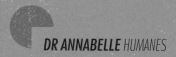

DR ANNABELLE *HUMANES*

NEW WAYS TO CELEBRATE

One of the aspects I enjoy most about life as an expat, as we experience family life in different countries around Europe, is discovering just how many interesting and fun cultural traditions there are for children to get involved with. Seeing how many different rituals and celebrations there are has also made me curious to learn, with my children, about traditions in countries we've never visited—and we've even been inspired to adopt some of these at home.

In almost every single culture, the first day of school is a very big deal. Parents might buy children new stationery and take cute pictures to mark the occasion. In Germany, where we moved to when my oldest was only one year old, it is a particularly special time. Schools organize welcoming ceremonies, and parents hold family parties for their children. The most iconic tradition of a child's first day at school in Germany is the *Schultüte* (school cone). The cone is usually crafted at home out of paper and filled by the family with lots of small treats for the child—from sweets to school supplies to toys. Sometimes the cone is as big as the child holding it! My children each made their own cone with the staff at their kindergarten. The cones symbolized their transition to school and remain treasured pieces of art, full of happy memories and displayed proudly in their bedrooms.

> **"On Japanese Children's Day, we made fish-shaped streamers and flew them outside our window."**

Embracing one tradition often means leaving another one behind. Until my early 20s, I lived in France, and one of my favorite days was April 1st, April Fool's Day. Known as *poisson d'avril* (April's fish), it definitely is a highlight in the calendar when you are a child. As well as the jokes and pranks adults play on each other, children, especially in school, draw and cut out small or large fish shapes and attempt secretly to attach them with sticky tape to the backs of their unsuspecting victims' sweaters or shirts. Braver children boldly plant the fish and shout proudly *"poisson d'avril!"* It is not uncommon for teachers and children to walk around school with fish taped to their backs all day.

I have discovered that, in Japan, they have a special Children's Day, a national holiday—where fish are also featured. A *koinobori* is a carp-shaped streamer flown in celebration every year on May 5. The carp is a symbol of energy, strength, and courage in Japan. Families make the streamers by drawing and decorating a fish shape on paper, fabric, or cloth. The fish are then hung on a pole or stick and left to flutter in the wind in honor of all children, in the hope that they will grow up healthy and strong. A *koinobori* can be made large or small, and they are relatively easy to create with your children at home and fly in your garden or outside your window to celebrate strong children and learn about Japan. We made these streamers during the very first COVID-19 pandemic lockdown to celebrate healthy and strong children all around the world.

Finally, have you ever thought about the traditions surrounding a child's first tooth loss? The fairy who collects the tooth from beneath the sleeping child's pillow, leaving a coin, is common in many countries, but she doesn't visit every place around the world. In France (and many Spanish-speaking South American countries), a little mouse or a rat comes instead. The tooth is often simply left on a bedside table, and the mouse creeps in to exchange it for a coin at nighttime. My children were puzzled when we moved to Germany from France and their classmates spoke about a fairy they had never heard of! In our house now, the mouse and fairy take turns to visit. Meanwhile, in Benin, Korea, and Cambodia, children losing a front tooth will throw it on the roof of their home. Parents in other cultures, for example, Malaysians or Aboriginal Australians, will bury their child's tooth to return it to the earth.

My favorite tradition has to be the German school cone. I am so glad my children got to experience such a special first day of school.

FARIBA SOETAN

RAISING CURIOUS KIDS

I used to love watching a show with my little ones called *Team UmiZoomie*, a cartoon that took a team of four superheroes on a journey around the world looking for baddies. There were always a few educational facts about the country they were in to entertain us!

Fast-forward several years, and my children need more than a few facts to keep them engaged and learning about the world around them. I want them to grow up to be not just informed but curious and open to new ideas and cultures. To do that, I try to expose them to stories about people, wherever they're based, to bring facts alive.

Books are always my go-to for introducing concepts that open children's minds to new experiences and realities. We used the picture book *The Name Jar* (see Resources, p.216, for details of books and shows mentioned) to explore what it might feel like to move from Korea to America and how the main character might have felt when the other children couldn't learn how to say her name properly. My eldest recently read *Little House on the Prairie*, first published in 1932, and as a consequence had heaps of questions about Indigenous people, who were often portrayed negatively in the book—but who, she was savvy enough to realize, obviously had their own story.

> **"I hope the books and experiences I expose my children to will help them question and be broad-minded."**

Movies and TV also challenge my children's ideas of the world. My middle daughter loves to watch a program where children from all over the country are invited to cook a dish that originates from where their parents come from. It's always interesting for her to see that even kids who appear white and she assumes are native to the UK can actually be immigrants. It helps her not only appreciate difference but also see life as a learning adventure.

EXPERIENCE THE JOY OUR WORLD HAS TO OFFER.

ACTION PLAN
Try It Out

Introduce your child to different cultural experiences from all over the world. Try out some books, films, music, and activities that you wouldn't usually consider.

MINIATURE GARDEN

Your child might like to create a Chinese garden or a Japanese zen garden in miniature. Research different garden styles online, then let them gather moss, pebbles, and other natural materials to create their own small-scale version inside a shallow box or on a tray.

POETRY

From narrative poetry to nursery rhymes, nonsense rhyme to the Japanese haiku, there is a type of poetry to delight every taste and age. Read poems out loud to your child and see whether you can find a collection you both enjoy, or you could even try writing a poem together.

MAKE SUSHI

If you enjoy eating sushi, your child might have fun making it with you, and may even be brave enough to taste the results. There are how-to videos and instructions available online, and you can even buy kits containing the necessary ingredients.

FAIRY TALES

You may be familiar with *Hansel and Gretel* from Germany and *Aladdin* from the Middle East, but there are plenty more traditional tales to introduce your child to from all over the world. Try *Baba Yaga* from Russia, *Bunbuku Chagama* from Japan, or go back to Ancient Greece for *Aesop's Fables,* including *The Tortoise and the Hare.* You could also read gender-swapped fairy tales (see Resources, p.216) in order to consider traditional roles in a new light.

EXHIBITIONS

Even children who don't usually enjoy art galleries might be inspired by a photography exhibition. The Natural History Museum's Wildlife Photographer of the Year touring exhibition showcases the stunning diversity of life on Earth. Some images can be viewed online.

CLASSICAL MUSIC

If classical music doesn't usually get a listen in your home, introduce your child to some accessible orchestral or choral pieces. Try *Carnival of the Animals* by the French composer Camille Saint-Saëns. Each movement represents a different animal, including a lion, elephant, and the most famous, a swan. Another classic is Russian composer Prokofiev's symphony for children *Peter and the Wolf,* in which music and a narrator bring the story to life.

FUN AND GAMES

Twenty-first-century playtime can be more exciting than ever before. Discover games and activities from all over the world that your child can enjoy with you and with friends.

Chess (India), Scrabble (America), Risk (France), Catan (Germany), Mahjong (China), and the ever-reliable jigsaw puzzle (Britain)—the contents of the family game cabinet originate from all over the globe. Open your child's eyes to how imports from other countries and cultures contribute to our everyday enjoyment and have fun seeing whether there are new pastimes you can adopt. By playing different games with your child—whether imaginative play or structured games—you teach them valuable social skills and demonstrate how they can make playtimes with friends a success, too.

INTERNATIONAL INTERESTS

Disney, IKEA, and fajitas are not the only imports we've absorbed seamlessly into our daily lives. Sports, hobbies, music, games, and cultural and family celebrations—many of our most life-enhancing and adrenalin fueled activities were invented elsewhere. We have New Zealand to thank for Zorbing (rolling around inside a giant transparent ball), the US for Laser Tag, and a Dutchman for the first inline skates. Origami from Japan, Mehndi (henna body art) from India, and even knitting, which is believed to have originated from the Middle East, provide creative outlets for many. If your child loves music, as well as international pop stars, why not listen to or play folk music (from the German word for people, *volk*) from regions and societies around the world; or country music from Tennessee; or Middle Eastern music with its distinctive cadences?

Many of our traditions are rooted in religious observation, such as the rituals observed around Eid, Diwali, or Hannukah, for example. You may give some your own twist, perhaps adopting ideas from elsewhere. Is there an Elf on the Shelf in your house between Thanksgiving and Christmas Eve, a custom started in America this century? The Easter Bunny is not in the Bible, but the chocolate eggs he piles into a basket or hides in the long grass are an important part of Easter celebrations for many children; the hiding of eggs is believed to have originated with the German "Easter Hare." You may take part in Chinese New Year without being Chinese, or have only a very tangential connection with Scotland or Ireland while celebrating Burns Night in January, or St. Patrick's Day in March. At Halloween, traditional forms of trick-or-treating have now become more standardized in many cultures.

PLAYING WELL

Taking part in social activities and enjoying sports, cards, and playground and other games teaches your child how to get along well with others, take turns, and be supportive as well as how to handle competition. Some children are happy to jump straight in to a game with a friend or a group. Others may need a little prompting from adults, who can start the game off and then back away once the children are hooked. If you have a shy, awkward, or anxious child, it can be more difficult for them to engage with peers. Playing a game they enjoy together—whether *Chutes and Ladders* or *What's the Time, Mr. Wolf?*—will teach them the basics of give and take and being a good winner or loser. Look for opportunities for them to socialize with friendly, open-hearted children to practice these skills further.

If your child doesn't know how to join in with a playground game, encourage them to observe what the other children are doing and then find a way in that fits. If they are playing store, for example, your child could arrive as a customer. Teach them not to criticize or jump in trying to alter things to their own taste, and to exit with grace and find something else to do if the others don't want them to join at that moment.

DR ANNABELLE *HUMANES*

GLOBAL PLAYGROUND

Discovering the world through games is a fun way to raise children's cultural awareness, as well as improve their geography.

Chat perché (perching cat), France This is a classic from my own French childhood. The "cat" has to catch the "mice" by touching them. When a mouse is caught, they swap roles. Mice can escape the cat by climbing up onto something—say, a step, bench, or swing. There are many variations of this game of Tag around the world. My children also play the German version, *Fangen* (catch), in which there is no safe "home" for children to rest.

Pilolo (time to search), Ghana A child is chosen to hide one little trinket, stone, or stick per player inside a designated area. That child becomes the timekeeper. When they shout *"pilolo!"* the others must start searching for a hidden item, which they take over the finish line as quickly as possible. The first to cross the line gets a point. The next child then hides the trinkets and becomes timekeeper, until everyone has had a turn. Children also sing songs while they search.

Luta de Galo (fight of the roosters), Brazil Each child must partner up with an opponent into whose pocket or belt they tuck a small piece of fabric. Holding their right arm across their chest and their left leg off the ground, they must try to grab their opponent's fabric piece while not letting their own one be captured. If they drop their right arm or let their left leg touch the ground, they're out.

> **"Games from different countries can give a global twist to playtime at home, school, or a birthday party."**

Finally, how about a different version of hopscotch? In *piko*, from the Philippines, the markings on the floor are made up of six squares, unlike the usual eight (or 10). In the Iranian *waylay*, the player must kick the stone into the next square (instead of tossing it).

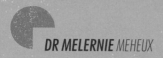

DR MELERNIE MEHEUX

TAKING PLAY SERIOUSLY

Play is a universal language of childhood that doesn't need to be taught and occurs across cultures. Play can be structured or free. As well as being fun, playing is essential for our children's emotional, cognitive, physical, creative, and language development.

Through play, children learn vocabulary, listening skills, and understanding. Playing games develops their imagination, confidence, and concentration. Children develop friendships, citizenship, social skills, and relatedness to others and the world as they play—and it allows them to safely learn from their mistakes. Play is a way for our children to communicate, just as using words is for adults. When a child is happily engaged in a game, their brain releases positive chemicals, such as oxytocin which helps them feel calm and safe in the world.

Parents can model play for children by remembering to play themselves—for example, by making time to watch a movie or listen to music, or by pursuing hobbies. It's also important that we encourage our children to play collaboratively with us, siblings, and local and international friends. Playing together strengthens relationships across global communities and families. Sharing quality time, and actively taking part in our children's play, helps to strengthen our bonds with them.

> **"Play is essential for development and is a way for children to communicate across cultures."**

With younger children, where possible, get fully involved, down to their level on the floor, playing face to face so that they see your expression. They can make games and activities from everyday resources, such as musical instruments out of kitchen utensils, or junk modeling from recyclables like cardboard and plastic. When you are playing with your child, it's important to let them take the lead, exploring and trying things out so that they can make mistakes and problem-solve. Structured games are good and so is free play. Asking a child what-if questions, such as "What if we tried to build a tower from ice cubes?" will foster their imagination and give you an opportunity to provide essential vocabulary as they answer and experiment. Independent play is also important, allowing children to come up with creative games and solutions all by themselves. With older children, you might play board games, such as Chess or Scrabble, or Charades to develop understanding of rules, cognition, and thinking skills—all while having fun!

Play is a form of escapism for all children and exists in a variety of forms. For teenagers, immersing themselves in a book, social media, or an online game with peers across the world are all forms of play. Children of all ages might also engage in physical activities, such as group sports. With increased concerns about obesity, reduced levels of physical exercise, and mental health problems, promoting such activities is a great way to help improve children's physical and emotional well-being. With younger children, you could make a game out of going for a walk together by playing "I spy" or spotting colors or objects. We can also go for walks with our dogs, go on bike rides, or join free park runs.

Parents often cite differences in their own experiences of play in comparison to their children's. The days of endless unsupervised play outdoors have disappeared, and with increased traffic in our communities, closures of public play settings, and increased parental anxieties about safety, there are reduced opportunities for outdoor community play. In several countries, schools have replaced playtime with standardized tests and test prep. Doing so increases pressure and toxic stress on children. However, studies show that playtime can actually help children learn and behave better, which is all the more reason for parents to take play seriously and be creative with play opportunities for their children. Article 31 of the United Nations Convention on the Rights of the Child enshrines children's rights to play—so let's get our children playing!

ACTION PLAN
Enjoy Yourselves

Play is a universal language that broadens children's minds and teaches vital skills. Help your child absorb information and understanding about the world and other people as they have fun playing.

PRESENTATION

Any activity that absorbs your child is play. If they love spending time on the computer and know how to use PowerPoint, they might like to make a presentation about something that interests them, for example, animals around the world; famous buildings; or a country of their choosing. They can proudly talk you through the slideshow afterward.

MAKE A POTION

Wizards and witches everywhere love to make magical potions. Collecting leaves, grass, and petals out and about to stir up in their big pot will put them in touch with their environment. A long twig can act as a magic wand. Make sure no one tastes the terrible concoction!

DRESS UP

Dressing up is a wonderful way for children to express their creativity and explore identity. Inspire them with information about national costumes around the world. Just a couple of accessories—a hat, necklace, or unexpected shoes—can send their imagination on a journey.

HANGMAN

Hangman is a simple game for any place, any time, and with older children it can be fun to play in a different language. The first player puts a dash for each letter in a word they want the other player to guess. They then draw one stroke of a hangman's noose and a stick man victim each time a wrong letter is guessed. The second player has to guess the mystery word before they get "hung."

PLAY DOUGH

Play dough can be made at home with flour, salt, water, oil, and food coloring. Children can use it to cut out or mold shapes, or if you're feeling adventurous, print or draw bold outlines of different countries and have them mold pretend relief maps, keeping within the borders.

SET A TIMER

Not all adults enjoy one-on-one imaginative play with children, but if your child is desperate to play a game with you, they will benefit from your undivided attention. Why not set a timer? By allocating around 20 minutes, you can give your child concentrated screen- and chore-free attention. Perhaps the timer's buzz could be part of the game, signaling the arrival of a new imaginary store assistant or pirate!

ONLINE CONNECTION

Social media and online gaming
can be forces for good in our global
society and are an integral part of
modern life. Help your child navigate
the digital world successfully.

For our children, online relationships are as normal as offline ones. From a young age, children become part of an online community that expands as they grow. Screen time can be a fun, enriching experience provided it's balanced with other activities children need for healthy development, such as physical exercise, time outdoors, creative play (dressing up, making up stories, drawing), socializing, reading, and sleep. They also need real-life role models (in addition to you, their most important role model), such as sports coaches or club leaders, not just online heroines or heroes. Your help and guidance are invaluable in helping your child thrive in the digital world.

MODERN CITIZEN

Time spent online can be educational, inspiring, and stimulating. It can also encourage good or useful behavior—your child might follow a celebrity's exhortation to save electricity more readily than yours. An app to identify nature; a TEDx talk; recipes; football tips; language learning—the internet can allow a child to independently follow an interest that has been sparked at home or at school. Connecting with friends online via games or social media is an important aspect of socializing for older children, widening and diversifying their pool of playmates, and online games help them develop their communication skills and the ability to play as part of a team.

For teenagers, engaging with reliable sources of news and debate online can stimulate their interest in current affairs and help them feel connected to their community and major social and political issues in the world, such as climate change. Teenagers might also take on board health messages, such as good eating habits, respectful relationships, and how to handle their emotions, more easily from peers and positive role models online than they would from parents. It's important to share screen time with your child and take an interest in what they do online at every age—not just to demonstrate that you care about them and their interests but also so you can guide them through the complexities of managing and interpreting online activity.

SUCCESSFUL SCREEN TIME

Establishing family rules around console, tablet, or phone use can help ensure your child maintains a healthy balance. Consider where in the house they are allowed to use screens (for example, shared areas, not bedrooms); at what times of day (after school, not at mealtimes); and in what situations (perhaps not when you have family visitors); as well as how often they need a jump-up-and-down activity break.

Instead of thinking purely about how many minutes or hours they devote to screens a day, it can be helpful to consider the purpose of their screen time. Quizzes, making or listening to music, finding instructions for a craft activity, reading a library book, chatting or messaging family and friends, writing a blog, making a video, learning some coding—the time allowed might vary according to what they are doing.

HIGH QUALITY

The key consideration is the quality of the media your child is engaging with. Help them analyze and reflect on their games and viewing from a young age. Wholly age-inappropriate content should be avoided, and ratings and reviews can help you figure out what falls into that category. When in doubt, sit with your child. In movie clips and games, are there positive messages about relationships, with the characters treating each other with respect, or does violence or a bad attitude win the day? Irony will

be lost on younger children, which can dramatically alter their interpretation of online videos. Does an app bombard you with ads or promote in-app purchases? How much data is it collecting about the user? If a celebrity is endorsing a product, discuss the fact that they might have been paid to do so.

Teenagers need to be sophisticated consumers, able to sift out reliable information from "fake news" and advertising, and appreciate the influence the media has in making us decide what is "normal" and "acceptable." Do sexualized images, violent imagery, and coarse language they see or hear online reflect people and behavior in real life, in the supermarket, or at school? Are discussion forums genuinely debating all opinions, or are they promoting biased or hateful attitudes around gender or sexuality, for example?

Talk through with your child why you follow who you do on social media. Consider together one of the YouTube channels or Instagram accounts your child follows and discuss the YouTuber or Instagrammer behind it—what's their motivation, and how are they trying to make you feel? Has that worked? For public figures, such as politicians and celebrities, explore together what attracts you or your child to them. How do you know whether the information posted about them is true or false? If something they say, whether directly on social media or via reporters, provokes a strong crowd reaction online, consider to what extent the reaction is justified.

GAMING

Some games, even for young children, are designed to be addictive, for example, in the way they don't allow users to save their progress when quitting. The adrenaline and frustration can be very hard to manage, even for adults, and will lead children to beg for "just 10 more minutes." These games are best avoided or restricted to short sessions so your child stays in control of their emotions. Encourage them to recognize feelings of crossness and frustration when they first emerge so they can step away from the screen before they build. Agree on how much time they have to play in advance, before they get sucked in—perhaps set a timer to go off at the end of the session.

Limit your younger child's online interactions to people they know in real life as they explore online behavior and learn to play well together. A Minecraft Player, for example, doesn't give anything away, so your child doesn't have the support

of facial cues or tone of voice to know whether someone's intent in a game is cheeky or malicious. A real-life relationship means they can discuss tactics face to face and figuree out together what's acceptable. Online bullying, where a group of players in a multiplayer game repeatedly kill or steal from another player, can be as upsetting as real-world bullying Help your younger child learn to be a good sport so that when, they start to play with people they don't know, they can carry these values forward and recognize and step away from poor online behavior.

Violent video games aren't suitable for younger children, who can't necessarily distinguish between fantasy and reality or understand the reasons for the violence in the game. If teenagers play video games that involve adult themes such as criminal activity or exploitation of women, it's important to explore these topics. How would we deal with feeling angry or upset in real life? Who are the victims—are they always the same gender or ethnicity? Help your child grow up respectful and tolerant of others in society, distinguishing between playing games for fun and relaxation and online behavior that can have a direct impact on the lives of fellow citizens.

JAMES MURRAY

POSITIVE FORCE

In 2019, the BBC published a story about a young man from Oslo named Mats Steen who died at the tragically young age of 25. Mats was severely disabled and led a life that had seemed sadly isolated, so his parents were surprised to be joined at the funeral by many of his close friends who they had never met. Right across Europe, candles were lit in his memory.

The family discovered Mats had enjoyed a rich social life as Lord Ibelin Redmoore in the role-playing game *World of Warcraft*. His parents had worried about the amount of time he spent online. But in a blog post Mats shared with his friends, he explained it was a place where "my handicap doesn't matter, my chains are broken and I can be whoever I want to be. In there I feel normal."

Much reporting on gaming and social media focuses on risks such as cyberbullying, grooming, and radicalization. But there's another side to the story—it really has never been easier to create connections.

This connectivity has also ushered in an era of hyper-transparency. A new discipline has emerged where citizen journalists tackle everything from corruption to war crimes. For example, within hours of the US Capitol riot in the dying days of the Trump administration, digital sleuths were notifying the FBI of rioters' identities. These investigators trawled a darker side of the web, including the misinformation channels digital platforms enable. But they also demonstrated how social media can be a positive force.

> *"Social media can be messy and frustrating—and a source of information and inspiration."*

For me, the corner of the internet that is "Climate Twitter" provides one of the most rewarding aspects of my professional life. There, people argue, joke, and comfort one another as they wrestle with the most important of topics. It is messy and magnificent—just like life itself.

MARVYN HARRISON

FINDING YOUR TRIBE

One of the uncontested beauties of the internet today is its ability to connect you to your tribe around the world with just a few taps on a screen. Not only can this benefit your child as they grow older and learn more about the world; it can also provide you with resources and connections to help you raise them. This is what you call being a digital citizen.

For example, Dope Black Dads was set up as a digital community to support Black fathers with their mental health, male parenting, and navigating the worlds of masculinity and fatherhood. Today, the Dope Black community operates across the US, UK, South Africa, and other territories around the world with large Black populations. The groups have also expanded to represent several intersections of Black communities, including mothers and queer and disabled groups who are focused on driving change.

Parents everywhere can easily create or join online communities that are dedicated to issues surrounding parenting and/or life. These types of groups are designed around group therapy, which encourages conversations about shared experiences, as well as coming together to support and

> **"I don't want my children to live in a world where they feel alone, and as digital citizens, they don't have to."**

heal collectively. Involvement can be a powerful way forward for children, too, for many things, including standing up for their beliefs; sharing their lived experiences; connecting with people who have similar passions; challenging situations that don't work for them; and learning new things and educating others.

When I grew up, if you had niche interests, you could have easily been bullied into losing or quitting your passions. Being a digital citizen opens the door to being part of broader communities and meeting more people like you.

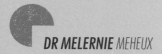

DR MELERNIE *MEHEUX*

A GOOD EXPERIENCE

In today's digital world, virtually all children access media via laptops, smartphones, tablets, consoles, and online television. In 2019, Ofcom reported that children aged 3 to 15 spend an average of 29 hours and 6 minutes per week online, while those aged 12 to 15 were reported to use online media for an average of 34 hours and 24 minutes per week—although those figures didn't include phone use, suggesting this was an underestimate. Children can spend more time online than sleeping or learning in school! It's important to bear in mind, however, that children are on screens for many different reasons, including homework and connecting with friends and family, and these experiences can be a positive and life-enhancing part of growing up as a global citizen. During the COVID-19 pandemic, online education and socializing became the norm.

Understandably, parents often worry that we don't yet fully know the impact that screen time has on children's physical and social development. We do know that there are advantages to children's screen time. One study into early childhood education reported positive benefits from watching the TV show *Sesame Street*. Children who watched it in preschool were found to perform better academically, in both primary and secondary school. Psychologists aren't saying that watching TV programs raises attainment in itself (the study didn't look at factors such as parental support for learning, or tuition), but we can reassure parents that it's okay to watch in moderation, as this has benefits and also offers parents and children enjoyment and respite. As screen time has become increasingly interactive, via educational apps and websites, it is likely to offer even more benefits.

As a psychologist, I often hear concerns from parents of older children about online gaming, particularly fighting games. Early research suggested fighting games desensitized children and encouraged use of aggression to resolve problems. However, over time, a number of flaws in the reporting of such studies have emerged. Many failed to control for variables, such as participants' exposure to adverse life experiences. Consequently, some researchers have since suggested that exposure to fighting games doesn't actually cause aggressive and violent behavior unless children are already exposed to this in their home life. Overall, the research suggests there are some harmful effects of game violence, but not for the majority of children, and there are a number of things that parents can do to keep their child's gaming healthy. These include ensuring games are age-appropriate, knowing who children are playing with online, and monitoring children's responses to gaming. Observing how children problem-solve and cope in real-life situations will give you a truer indication of how they are developing than their online gaming reactions will. You can also encourage game-free times in the home, physical exercise, and one-on-one and family time.

While the jury is still out on the long-term impact of excessive

screen use, research clearly tells us how we can put things in place to make spending time online a healthy experience. In particular, by thinking about what media children use, and how and when they access it. Monitor age requirements for specific games, websites, and social media apps but also look at developmental readiness. Your child might be the right chronological age for an app, but are they ready emotionally?

"Time spent online has advantages for children provided we help them manage it in a healthy way."

Explain to children why you make decisions to keep them safe. We can also monitor sleep patterns, friendships, and levels of engagement at school. We can teach children to navigate social media safely, be kind, recognize online bullying, and share worries with adults. We can also model tech-free family time, be present in the background, and have social media contracts (see p.185) outlining rules and expectations.

ACTION PLAN
Play Well Online

Support your child as they become a good digital citizen, capable of using the internet in a rewarding and responsible way that will increase their positive connection with the rest of the world.

CHECK IT OUT

Talk to your child about their viewing and, if in doubt, check whether something they are interested in is appropriate for their age and stage. Try commonsensemedia.org and kids-in-mind.com for age-based reviews and ratings. For advice on staying safe generally on the internet, go to staysafeonline.org.

EXERCISE CHOICE

Take advantage of streaming services by broadening the scope of your child's viewing. If they are a fan of Disney animation, for example, try French director Michel Ocelot's movie *Azur & Asmar, the Princes' Quest*, or some age-appropriate Japanese anime from Studio Ghibli.

COLLABORATE

Online games are a great opportunity to teach your child the skills to collaborate well. If you join in with what they enjoy doing, for example, by playing console games with them or building a world together in Minecraft, you can guide them as you have fun.

FIND A PURPOSE

If your child spends a lot of time mindlessly browsing the internet, encourage them to use online resources in a more purposeful way. You could take a shared interest and explore it together, thinking how you could make use of your findings in real life. For example, if you both enjoy baking, check out Pinterest for fun cake ideas or watch cake decorators on YouTube and have a go at making something special yourselves. Help your child learn to sift through and apply information.

MAKE CONNECTIONS

A supportive online forum can be a lifesaver for a teenager who struggles to find like-minded peers at school. At www.childline.org young people can share feelings around all sorts of things, including sexuality and gender identity via moderated message boards.

FAMILY CONTRACT

There is no one-size-fits-all rule for screen time—what works for another family might not be right for yours. Involve your child in figuring out a family "contract" around when and how they—and you—use different platforms and access different types of content. Make sure your child knows they can talk to you about anything upsetting and ensure your teenager knows the law around sexting. Set up parental controls as appropriate.

EXPLORE TOGETHER

There is so much to discover about the world we live in. Build your child's knowledge and understanding of other people and places as they grow into a fully fledged global citizen.

LET'S GO

Collecting shells on a sun-drenched beach. Watching a gibbon swing through the forest. Eating tacos with fingers. Uncover the wonders of our world and its citizens.

Real-life travel can be eye-opening and mind-expanding for children, as they see, hear, and feel sights, sounds, and emotions they've never imagined. A desert island or rainforest doesn't need to be part of the itinerary, however. Children can be at their happiest vacationing near home, enjoying a more familiar climate and diet but seeing life from a new angle as they watch the stars from a sleeping bag on a camping trip, for example. Exploring the more exotic corners of the Earth can be done via books, TV shows, and the internet as well as conversations and storytelling.

FUN FACTS

It's easy to forget as adults how we take our knowledge for granted, and with a proliferation of misinformation available at the playground and online, from the Flat Earth Society upward, you can't assume that children know facts we consider basic. Supplement their school learning with some exploration of your own. Did they know that Africa is in all four hemispheres? France, with its scattered national territories, covers more time zones than Russia. There are no rivers in Saudi Arabia. The Greek National Anthem is based on a poem with 158 verses. See what captures your child's imagination and investigate from there. Perhaps you could have a day learning about rivers—the longest river (the Nile, 4,132 miles [6,695 km] long), the shortest (the Roe, 200 ft [61 m] long), the animals that live in them (not just fish, but freshwater turtles and pink-skinned Amazon River dolphins, too). You could even join in with World Rivers Day in September.

Asia, Africa, North America, South America, Antarctica, Europe, Oceania—ask your child to pick a continent. Find out what countries are in it, and choose one to investigate. What can you discover about its geography—is it flat or mountainous; are there lakes or beaches? Do they have volcanoes, earthquakes, typhoons? Perhaps you could research the national diet and base your meals around that for a day. Italy might be a popular choice, but is there more to it than pasta, pizza, and gelato? Help your child figure out what time Italians have breakfast, tea, go to school. For leisure, you could try out an Italian movie. What religion might your imaginary family be? Do they wear the same sorts of clothes as you? See whether you have anything suitable in the dress-up box. Investigating Italian fashion might spark an interesting conversation with your older child around the dangers of national stereotyping.

Sticker books containing flags of the world, quizzes, or a jigsaw puzzle naming counties or countries can be fun ways for children to absorb geographical knowledge effortlessly. Equipping them with basic know-how about the world will whet their appetite for future discoveries.

DEEP DIVE

Small explorations can be as absorbing as world-scale ones. Does your child love to collect something, such as feathers? Find out about the birds the feathers came from. Maybe they migrate in winter—where do they go? Your child might like to catalog their collection, listing the colors, smells, sounds, textures, and—where appropriate!—tastes. As well as teaching them about the world they live in, exploring and collecting encourages children's creativity. To sharpen your child's observation skills, try this: when you return from somewhere you've been together—even just the supermarket—write down 10 things each of you saw or experienced there. It will be interesting to see how your lists differ. Learning to apply a keen eye to their immediate surroundings will help your child note the contrasts when you travel elsewhere.

FARIBA SOETAN

INSPIRING
ENCOUNTERS

My daughters were learning at school recently about different festivals that people around the world, including some classmates, celebrate. We decided to take their education one step further by marking Chinese New Year at home—although not for the full 15 days! We wore red to symbolize good luck and researched Lunar New Year traditions, discovering that we were entering the Year of the Ox. We also watched on Netflix Ang Lee's groundbreaking movie from 2000, *Crouching Tiger, Hidden Dragon*. For my three impressionable young girls, it was fabulous to see a "princess" sporting incredible ninja moves and rebelling against the idea of a forced marriage. These moves, along with questions about Chinese emperors and an interest in traditional Chinese silk costumes, featured heavily throughout the next week. My partner and I were delighted for our daughters to see an empress heroine who wasn't white.

Learning doesn't always have to feature faraway places. On a recent walk, my children were complaining that they were bored. We decided to run a competition where they would each take photos of five interesting things while we were out and explain what they represented to them. The friendly sibling rivalry encouraged them to see the familiar park through a different lens. My five-year-old began pointing out the overlapping shadows that the bare branches of the oak trees cast over the ground; my seven-year-old noticed the collage of colors the wildflowers

> **"We made spring rolls and dumplings for a special Chinese New Year celebration dinner."**

displayed, and looked them up when we got home; while my oldest was captivated observing different insects, finding their most camera-friendly angle. What started out as a normal excursion turned out to be an educational and inspiring day.

DR ANNABELLE HUMANES

TRAVEL IS AN EDUCATION

"Schools don't show you the world. They just show you a bunch of careers," said Michelle Obama. It is with this principle in mind that my family and I subscribe to the spirit of "worldschooling," an educational movement that often involves traveling as a family and using the trips to enhance the child(ren)'s education. While we do not worldschool year-round—our kids are in regular school—we do like to travel whenever possible.

Travel is part of our family's identity. I am French. My husband is Portuguese. We have lived in the UK and Germany. Just to visit their grandparents, my children need to travel for half a day at least. We believe that travel is the best education we could give our children. We have always taken them everywhere and never thought of traveling less when we became parents. Traveling together has been one of the best things we

could ever have done—even worth the vomiting virus we caught in Brazil and a particularly stressful hospital stay in Italy.

Travel has taught our children humility. Experiences they have found exceptional—such as visiting Frida Kahlo's house, which was a dream come true for my nine-year-old European girl—make them feel fortunate, and they have learned to share their stories sensitively.

> **"Traveling together has been one of the best things we could ever have done—despite the challenges."**

Travel has taught them to be flexible, adaptable, and resilient. Sleeping on the floor on blankets and pillows was a feature of our early travels with babies and toddlers. I remember how my then-six-year-old's resilience was tested to the limit the first time she traveled without us, on a minor-accompanied service, returning from her grandparents' house on a long train trip.

Our adventures have opened their taste buds to so many new flavors. We never pick a restaurant for its children's menu. There is always something to be had, even if it is just from the grown-up plates. My eldest tried chicken hearts, a delicacy many Brazilian children love, without even flinching when it was offered to her in a restaurant in Brazil. *Nopales* (cactus) tacos also made it into the children's bellies during a stay in Mexico.

Travel has given them wonderful cultural awareness, independence, and linguistic abilities. The morning my eight-year-old returned from a walk clutching a basket of eggs she'd been given by our landlady—after chatting with her in a language of which she only knew a few words—it all felt worth it.

Travel is never about how far we can go. A camping trip to a nearby lake is just as fun as a flight to another destination in Europe. Real-life check: some of the situations we've lived through were incredibly stressful at the time, as any parent can imagine, but I would do it all over again for the amazing memories and the lessons we have learned.

JEN PANARO

CARRIED AWAY

Reading and cooking with my boys are two of my favorite ways to spend time with them. You can imagine my delight when my younger son picked out a really great picture book from the library that highlighted a young boy sharing an important cultural food with his friends, which also included a recipe in the back of the book for that special meal.

While we can't always travel the world, we can explore other cultures through our books and bellies. I've seen many picture books that incorporate authentic eating experiences and the recipes to make those special dishes. I've included a few of our favorites in Resources (see p.216). I love that making new foods with my kids offers an opportunity to spend time together as well as honing their cooking skills and exposing them to elements of other cultures. Kids begin to understand how their home and neighborhood are tiny elements of a large and diverse world.

ACTION PLAN
Have an Adventure

A small new experience can be a huge adventure for a child. As well as taking up opportunities to travel to unfamiliar places, be adventurous close to home, too.

NIGHT WALK

Take a flashlight and head out after dark with your family to see how different the world looks and feels at night. Do some stargazing and tell your child about the different constellations. From moths to urban foxes, see which animals venture out when the sun has gone down.

FESTIVAL

Camping overnight at a family festival or even just visiting on a day pass can introduce your child to a host of new sights, sounds, and sensations. Many offer all sorts of experiences from music, theater, and crafts to circus acts, fort building, and bushcraft. Prepare well for your trip and take earplugs if there will be loud music.

WATCH THE SUN RISE

Set your alarm extra early one spring or summer morning and make your way to a special place to watch the sun come up. It could be the top of a nearby hill, a street with a great view, or even the beach. You might want to take a picnic breakfast with you.

TREASURE HUNT

Most children love a treasure hunt, and there are a lot of forms this can take. For younger children, let them make their own treasure by painting pebbles that you then hide in a garden, park, or area of woodland for them to spot and collect, with a reward once they've gathered them all in. For older children, write clues or give them photographs of local landmarks at unusual angles; have them visit each one and check it off, with your home—and some treasure—at the very end of the trail.

PICK YOUR OWN

Even in big cities, there are often pick-your-own farms within reach, and these make a great day out for the whole family to harvest their favorite fruits and vegetables. Visit in strawberry season if you want to make jam, or gather apples in fall.

OUTDOOR CHALLENGE

If you love outdoor adventures, these don't have to stop once you become a parent. Taking part in activities and sports from hiking and cycling to sailing and paddleboarding can be more challenging with children but also extra special. Try online resources such as getoutwiththekids.com for tips, destinations, and product advice for family fun.

NEED TO
KNOW

The more your child understands about
world history and politics, the better
equipped they will be to understand why
and how life-changing decisions are made.

Does your child know who the president is? Could they tell you why there are photos in the history books of Elizabeth II's coronation but not of Elizabeth I's? Do they know who collects the trash bins each week and how this is paid for? Would they say they live in a poor country or a prosperous one, and what do they think about free speech?

KEY CONCEPTS

It's easy to give a flippant answer when asked, "What's a politician?" and your response will depend on the age of your child. Introduce them gradually to key concepts such as politics (the people and processes that determine how we live our lives), representative democracy (all citizens having equal right to vote for the people who make legislation), and what makes up a state (the legislature, executive, and judiciary). Explain that there are local politicians as well as national ones, and who is in power where you are. Direct and indirect taxation will be invisible to your child, but a shortage of school textbooks or new play equipment in the park won't be, so help them understand the links between voters' decisions and outcomes on the ground.

Most children don't consider themselves lucky to go to school.

However, older children in particular may appreciate the ability to read and make independent choices based on information they have access to and can interpret. In 2018, around 260 million children worldwide did not attend school—nearly one-fifth of the global population in that age group. The COVID-19 pandemic has worsened this figure. According to Oxfam, 781 million adults worldwide are illiterate—two-thirds of these are women. Gender inequality exists throughout the world—from the gender pay gap and an unequal share of unpaid care work to child marriage and physical and sexual violence, including female genital mutilation. In 18 countries, husbands can legally stop their wives from working.

Oxfam notes that the 22 richest men in the world have more wealth than all the women in Africa. World poverty is in decline; however, 10 percent of the world's population still lives in extreme poverty, struggling to access basic needs such as water, sanitation, health care, and education. We are fortunate to have access to clean drinking water, flushing toilets, and health care. However, there is also extreme deprivation in rich countries. In the US, nearly 11 million children live in poverty, and this is expected to increase.

WHERE WERE YOU WHEN ...?

Our parents might remember where they were at 9:32 a.m. Eastern Daylight Time, July 20, 1969, when Neil Armstrong landed on the moon; or in 1963 when US President John F. Kennedy was shot. For us, a chillingly memorable date might be September 11, 2001, when terrorists attacked the World Trade Center complex in New York—or the joyful day in 1989, November 9, when the Berlin Wall fell, opening the way to German reunification. These moments act as backdrops to our interpretation of current affairs without our necessarily realizing, but of course, our children don't have this or any frame of reference. Depending on their school's curriculum, they might never even study any modern history. Knowing what came before the present moment, from empire building to the Cold War, is central to understanding why people and governments behave as they do. Parents can help demystify the context and times we live in.

An understanding of the role religion plays in different regimes and people's lives is also key to fathoming how the world works. Faith is a force for good for billions of people, meeting spiritual needs and promoting positive values and actions. However, it is often religious conflict or the extremist factions of religious groups that hit the news headlines. Acts of intolerance, violence, and discrimination committed in the name of religion have increased around the world over the past decade and affect almost every religious group.

Whether or not your family is religious, help your child develop a sense of the breadth and diversity of religious belief and practice, beyond the often reductive reporting of news organizations. Christianity and Islam are the world's most widely practiced religions (32.8 percent identify as Christian and 22.5 percent as Muslim), and these dominate in Europe, the Americas, Africa, and Russia. Discover where in the world other religions dominate, such as Buddhism, Judaism, and Sikhism. Would it surprise your child to know that worldwide, 11.8 percent identify as atheist or agnostic, and if so, would they expect that number to be smaller or larger?

In around 30 countries—republics as well as monarchies—heads of state must belong to a specific religion. The United States of America was the world's first explicitly secular nation, although since 1956, the official US motto has been "In God we trust." Many countries' constitutions are ambiguous, as while they grant religious freedom and separate church and state, they privilege the state religion in some respects. Religious freedom, where it exists, is often hard-won, and the scars of conflict run deep.

FEED THEIR CURIOSITY

Current affairs magazines and TV shows aimed at children can inform your child about how the world works. Perhaps this will set them thinking about issues close to home, such as the lack of social mobility or the need for food banks in spite of a welfare state. Or maybe it will help them contrast our freedoms with restrictions elsewhere and think more deeply about the liberties we enjoy, such as freedom of speech—while considering where the line falls between free expression and slander or incitement of violence. What does your child think about different styles of governments, such as monarchy, republic, or dictatorship, as in North Korea (one of 50 countries around the world that has a dictator)? Your teenager might like to reflect on the difference between patriotism and nationalism or discuss whether richer countries should give financial aid to poorer countries. Some believe spending a percentage of national

income on overseas development aid is basic humanitarianism; others think it stops countries from building their own solutions and that we should invest in infrastructure for mutual benefit, enabling developing countries to become independently prosperous.

Globalization has made the world seem smaller. Countries need to work together if they are to successfully tackle some of the challenges faced by humans everywhere, such as climate change, pandemics, and economic injustice. According to the UN, every year, 1.3 billion tons of food are wasted—as some 2 billion people suffer from hunger and malnutrition. Yet collaboration is difficult, because despite all our connections, the world is still an enormous place, made up of vastly differing regimes informed by what can often appear alien values. To what extent a power that believes liberal democracy is a superior form of governance should try to impose its own values on other regimes is hotly debated—when are interventions, from naming and shaming, to economic sanctions, to military force, justified? And when do the means justify the ends? Exploring these very big ideas with your child, even in very small ways, can open their eyes to the complexities those in positions of power have to grapple with.

MARVYN HARRISON

POLITICAL AWAKENING

When you're a global citizen, there is no such thing as an isolated political incident. It is our job as parents to try to help our children understand how politics can affect everyday life. Perhaps a politician attempting to seize power in a country thousands of miles away has led ultimately to a new refugee kid in your child's class. As global citizens, children need to be aware of how the systems we live within impact not only us and our classmates and neighbors but larger populations, too. We can help them grow to understand how different types of leadership around the world, as well as the way different governments operate, have a huge impact on everything from work-based migration to poverty and people's rights and freedoms.

Being a parent is a great opportunity to develop or rediscover your own political education along with your child. Helping my 13-year-old nephew

understand some of these ideas involved first of all familiarizing him with certain countries and the political ideology of each one. I really wanted him to understand the practical implications of politics and how they might show up in his life as a teenager. I had him draw up a big chart on a sheet of paper. Starting with Europe, we listed every country, along with its population size, dominant religion, political ideology, and whether it had an active monarchy.

> **"I want my son to grow up understanding how political concepts connect to real life."**

This exercise created a very interesting conversation where we both discovered many things I just had forgotten. I also never knew that there are 12 sovereign monarchies in Europe. Seven are kingdoms—Denmark, Norway, Sweden, the United Kingdom, Spain, the Netherlands, and Belgium. Andorra, Monaco, and

Liechtenstein are principalities, while Luxembourg is a Grand Duchy. The Vatican City is a theocratic state ruled by the Pope. I had no idea what a Grand Duchy was (it's a country whose head of state is a Grand Duke or Grand Duchess), nor a theocratic state (it's a state where officials rule by divine guidance, and the legal system is based on religious law.)

We found learning together a great connection point for our ongoing relationship, and we now have a foundation for a discussion each time we speak. Try this exercise with your kids to help them learn the appropriate terms and start to understand how broad political concepts connect to lived experience. Feel free to begin on a smaller scale, perhaps with just a few of the countries that surround the one you live in.

For younger children, a great strategy I have found is to buy a world map and mark with a pin any countries your child has been to—even if it's just the one they live in. My son is five and has visited six countries, which makes it fun and memorable for him to point them all out on the map. In addition to teaching him the country names, each time we look at the map, I share one fact about a country—anything from telling him that it has a king or a queen to getting him to repeat the name of its president. I have found that when you make learning of individual facts fun and memorable, they stick. My son loves to shout the country names after me, louder and louder each time. This is a method that has worked for me, but consider the personality of your child and allow them to lead the learning.

My goal is for my son to remember each country and be able to use at least one interesting fact about it to strike up a conversation with someone who comes from there. At a more advanced age, he will be able to connect his understanding of the facts we've absorbed and use these as a starting point for discussion. I want him to learn not to make assumptions but to be able to have a sensitive discussion with another global citizen about the place they come from. I hope he will have enough understanding about different political regimes to be compassionate and proactive about the challenges other citizens face.

JAMES *MURRAY*

ECONOMY
ECOLOGY

Economics has often been disparaged as "the dismal science"—the discipline at the root of a technocratic and bloodless approach to life and politics—but economics is about so much more than GDP. The future of civilization depends upon it.

The word comes from the Greek *oikos*, which translates loosely as family, property, or home, and *nomos*, which means accounts. Economics is the practice of analyzing our collective home, of striving to account for the world around us and how it is ordered—or not. As such, economics is at the heart of the environmental and political challenges that will define children's lives this century.

Economics and ecology are twins, etymologically and philosophically. The past few decades have been shaped by an unresolved dichotomy. We've seen the fastest improvement in global living standards in history. We've also seen escalating climate impacts, together with debilitating erosion of the soils, fisheries, oceans, and watercourses—our natural capital—that sustain the global economy. It is unclear how long this situation can persist.

The big question is whether we can reorder our home to put it on a sustainable footing, developing a circular and clean economy where inputs and outputs are in balance, where stocks and flows are stable.

> **"Economics is at the heart of the environmental and political challenges defining this century."**

There are causes for cautious optimism. Alongside encouraging clean tech innovation, there is a growing understanding that a healthy economy is built on a healthy environment. One cannot survive without the other. Natural capital is as important as financial capital. Economy and ecology are intertwined. This is the economics children need to know. It is an economics about the only home we've got.

DIVE IN TO LIFELONG LEARNING AND CREATE A BETTER FUTURE.

ACTION PLAN
Educate and Inform

Sparking your child's interest in how the world works will enable them to become lifelong learners, developing the understanding and knowledge they will need to play an active role in society.

ARTIFACTS

Bring history to life with pictures and artifacts—real or replica. Your child might play with a Viking sword, for example, or display a wartime poster on their wall. Make a point of spotting things of historical significance in your environment, such as plaques and war memorials.

PAY A VISIT

Does your child understand how local government works? Visit your county town or City Hall so they can see for themselves where many of the decisions surrounding things that affect them, such as schools, libraries, and transportation, are made by the council. Visit your capital city, too, if possible, so they can see where government meets.

LEARN BY HEART

Challenge your child to learn something by heart—for example, the names of the first 10 presidents of the United States or countries in Africa. It's a fun party trick for them and also gets them into the habit of holding knowledge, which gives them a useful base for future learning.

READ ALL ABOUT IT

There are some fantastic magazines aimed at children that will keep them up to date with world developments and current affairs. Your child's school or PTA might take out a subscription so the whole class can benefit. Try *National Geographic Kids*, for example. With your older child, watch the news together sometimes and talk through what you see.

FACTORY TOUR

The worlds of business and economics can seem abstract to children. To bring them to life, why not take a factory tour? There are factories around the country that you can visit, sometimes for free. This will show your child the physicality of manufacturing and production.

MONEY SAVVY

Help your child learn the value of money. They can allocate weekly pocket money to two different mason jars, one labeled "spending" and the other "saving." In the "saving" jar, they can save up for something they really want, figuring out how long this will take and eventually make a special outing to buy it. Older children can open a bank account and learn to use a debit card responsibly, keeping track of their balance.

FRESH EYES

Children assume their "normal" is everybody's normal. Give them an insight into what "normal" looks like for other people and help them see their world with fresh eyes.

Have you ever pretended to be a tourist in your hometown or city—or a visitor from another planet? It can be enlightening and fun to consider familiar places from a new perspective. A town may seem small or big depending on whether you are arriving from a hamlet or a city. To see other people's views in a new light, children need to gain some understanding of what is at the root of their opinions.

TOLERANCE AND IMAGINATION

It's easy to believe other people are "crazy" for some of their views and actions—such as loving or disliking a politician or celebrity and what they stand for. Traditional and social media often support and fuel these beliefs that "we" are sensible and "they" are mad, but that politician's supporters are no more or less rational than those in the opposing camp. They are just as likely (or unlikely) to be doing what they consider to be the best for their community. Humans instinctively gather in groups, and to reinforce their group bond, they might condemn those who don't fit in. Even people who believe tolerance is vital can be intolerant of those who don't feel the same! Help your child think and learn about where another

person's point of view and subsequent actions stem from. If they understand why somebody does something, while they may still condemn the decision, they are more likely to have empathy for the human being who has made it.

Accepting those with profoundly different beliefs from our own can be difficult, especially if they throw our entire identity into question, such as faith groups who deny homosexuality. Part of accepting otherness is accepting the right of other people to think differently, although that does not mean having to agree with or enable those views. Help your child stand up for what they believe, while considering what it's like to be somebody other than themselves. Sometimes they will need to walk toward people with conflicting views, not expect them to come to them. Perhaps those people share the same values but have a different way of expressing them. Perhaps bringing together two conflicting viewpoints will bring about not just small adjustments to existing ways of thinking but brand-new solutions.

It's not always comfortable to see life from a different perspective, but the ability to think flexibly and be resilient in adjusting to new ideas will stand your child in good stead for their future, which we can't yet imagine.

DR MELERNIE *MEHEUX*

EMBRACING THE NEW

The way in which children see the world is shaped by their experiences and their interactions with the people around them. Parents and caregivers play a vital role in influencing the value judgments and beliefs children hold about themselves and others.

Having spent time teaching four-year-olds, I've often seen firsthand just how influenced young children are by the actions of the adults in their lives. One particular afternoon during "international food day," I noticed a child looking suspiciously at some grape halves. He was offered some to try but declined repeatedly. His teacher tried a range of techniques to entice him, but still he refused—until he saw me eat several, at which point he tried one tentatively then ate handfuls in quick succession! As children grow older, while they are still open to adult views, they are more likely to be influenced by peers. Your child developing a diverse friendship group is to be encouraged and celebrated, as this exposes them to alternative worldviews.

To help your child be open to new viewpoints and experiences as they grow up, let them see you explore your environment, asking questions and encouraging them to do the same. Be genuinely curious. Trying new foods or storybooks may seem like small acts, but adult modeling of acceptance of differences ultimately extends to tolerance and social harmony. I have witnessed children be exposed to a range of cultural

> **"A child's worldview is shaped by the everyday experiences they have and their interactions with adults."**

experiences, including international cooking sessions and global stories, and they have loved the opportunity to escape and immerse themselves in new worlds. With the support of adults, children will embrace new experiences and become inquisitive and inclusive global citizens.

JESS PURCELL

FACTS, NOT FEAR

As members of the world community, our children must learn to make their decisions and their arguments based on facts, not fear, and to communicate those facts with respect and compassion.

The simple problem-solving steps of the scientific method can help them do this. Understanding the following steps can help your child break down all sorts of tricky decisions and arguments:

• Establish a question that needs to be answered.

• Make observations about the subject in question.

• Create a plausible hypothesis, or answer, to the question based on observations.

• Test the hypothesis using logical, step-by-step procedures.

• Analyze the results of your test and draw conclusions based on findings.

A critical component of this skill set is teaching your child how to work with someone who disagrees with their viewpoint. Explain to your child that the first step in effective communication is to listen in order to understand why someone feels the way they do. They should try to find common ground so that they can slowly move forward together. Remind your child that even after establishing evidence-based conclusions, their friend may still choose to disagree and that they have the right to do so.

"You can teach your child to make thought-through decisions based on facts and rooted in respect."

Practicing with a sibling can be a great place to start. My children recently disagreed on where to play together. My daughter wanted outside, while my son preferred to stay indoors. Having them ask each other why got to the heart of the matter. My son liked inside because that's where his dinosaurs live. When my daughter realized the disagreement was about toys, not location, she suggested they bring the dinosaurs out to explore the yard—and the problem was solved!

MARVYN HARRISON

OWNING YOUR IDENTITY

The future is not guaranteed to be the way we imagine it. What we do know is that the generation we are raising today will have more information than we ever did, or our parents' generation did before us. The dominance of the internet and digital experiences means someone thousands of miles away is accessible in a few clicks and a follow, and this will create a much more interconnected lived experience for our children.

It is my belief that identity will evolve away from nationality, gender, race, and religion and will increasingly be based on passions and values. Being a global citizen, and after reading this book, you understand that the human race is deeply connected—that connection is underutilized because we draw lines between ourselves and others, based on ideas steeped in colonialism, imperialism, and religious supremacy. If you are born in the Republic of Ireland, statistically you are more likely to be Catholic versus being born in India, where you are most likely to be Hindu. Neither is right nor wrong, but we shouldn't make assumptions about someone, or determine their value, potential, character, and morals, based around systems they are born in to.

Global citizens will wear their own values on their chests proudly and invite people in to their lives on the basis of who they are and their shared interests—not labels. Even if the future isn't a utopia, and there

> **"Global citizens have their own personal approach to life, but not one that adversely impacts others."**

may arrive times when your identity as a global citizen comes under attack, there is a power in owning who you are regardless of external expectations, views, and opinions. That is what we want to give the next generation the confidence to do.

JAMES MURRAY

THE START OF HISTORY

About halfway through my childhood, history ended—or so a lot of clever people thought. The central premise of Francis Fukuyama's famous 1989 essay *The End of History?*—that liberal democracy had brought centuries of debate about the preeminent form of governance to an end—was widely shared and hugely influential. It really did seem as if democratic government and responsible capitalism could harness the best parts of globalization and deliver peace and prosperity in perpetuity.

It didn't quite work out like that. Since then, worldwide we've had countless wars and atrocities, two devastating economic crashes, a resurgence of illiberal authoritarianism, and escalating climate and global health crises. We've also experienced a dramatic decline in the number of people living in poverty, staggering technological progress, considerable (if distressingly incomplete) advances in civil rights, and the start of a green industrial revolution. Reports of history's demise were somewhat exaggerated.

What happens next is anyone's guess. Based on current emissions trends, we could see 5 degrees Fahrenheit of warming this century, which would unleash myriad dystopian impacts. Conceivably, many countries would respond to

> *"Young people have a huge say in determining which path we travel as they engage fully with the world."*

such environmental stresses by retreating into the suffocating embrace of aggressive nationalisms. Equally, you can look at the wind turbines and electric vehicles of the modern age, the continuing allure of liberalism and multilateralism, and ever greater levels of global connectivity and envisage a world where societies unite around the shared global mission of averting climate catastrophe.

Young people are going to have to be resilient, flexible, and innovative. But history is there to be made.

ACTION PLAN
Look Forward

What will your child be like in 10 or 20 years' time? As well as following your natural instinct to protect them, start to prepare them for the future, ready to be a force for good in a changing world.

GENDER NEUTRAL

Parents can help break down gender barriers. Remember to praise your son's sensitivity and commend your daughter's assertiveness. Make sure that your older daughter helps mow the lawn and your son does his share of the laundry. Expectations around gender roles are set by you, not them.

CRACK A JOKE

Humor can help us cope with adversity and defuse difficult situations. Finding the funny side of a situation can also be empowering and disconcert a bully. Enjoy jokes and laugh at your foibles and at life's absurdities with your child as you cultivate valuable social skills.

AIM FOR IMPERFECTION

Children will need to be creative in the workplaces of the future. Encourage this by allowing them free time and space and permission to fail. Give them the tools to fix mistakes for themselves, instead of doing this for them, and make sure they keep expectations realistic.

GRATITUDE DIARY

Help your child develop a positive outlook by learning to appreciate what they have. They might like to keep a gratitude diary, noting down once a day or once a week the good things that have happened to them, however small. This can give them a balanced view of life's ups and downs, which can be particularly helpful during the teenage years. It can also help them share positivity with others and problem-solve as they start to discover what makes them happy.

LET'S GIVE IT A GO

Your everyday language can have a big impact on your child's attitude to life. Hearing you say "I will try," "Let's give it a go," "I wonder," "I'm curious," "Imagine if ..." can awaken their appetite for discovery and also let them know that mistakes are not the end of the world.

MAKE A TIME CAPSULE

If your child is passionate about saving the world, why not create a time capsule so that as an adult they can reconnect with those emotions and their childhood authenticity? They could include a letter to their future self as well as pictures or articles from magazines that inspire them and toys or objects that are meaningful. Decorate a shoebox to use as the capsule and bury it deep in a cupboard or attic.

BIBLIOGRAPHY

BOOKS

Conflicted—Why Arguments Are Tearing Us Apart and How They Can Bring Us Together by Ian Leslie (Faber)

What Every Parent Needs to Know by Margot Sunderland (DK)

Why I'm No Longer Talking to White People About Race by Reni Eddo-Lodge (Bloomsbury)

Wish We Knew What to Say by Dr. Pragya Agarwal (Dialogue Books)

World Politics in 100 Words by Eleanor Levenson, illustrated by Paul Boston (Quarto)

REFERENCES

LOVE THE PLANET

19 Temperature increase
public.wmo.int/en/media/press-release/new-climate-predictions-assess-global-temperatures-coming-five-years

19 Rise in sea level
sealevel.nasa.gov/understanding-sea-level/by-the-numbers

20 Extinction
www.un.org/sustainabledevelopment/blog/2019/05/nature-decline-unprecedented-report

29 Carbon footprint
www.nature.org/en-us/get-involved/how-to-help/carbon-footprint-calculator/#:~:text=The%20average%20carbon%20footprint%20for,under%202%20tons%20by%202050.

29 Household emissions
www.pbs.org/newshour/science/5-charts-show-how-your-household-drives-up-global-greenhouse-gas-emissions#:~:text=We%20found%20that%20over%2020,figure%20is%20closer%20to%2080%25.

34 Pesticides worst offenders
www.ewg.org/foodnews/dirty-dozen.php

BE A FRIEND

61–62 Social attitudes on gender roles
www.cnbc.com/2018/12/13/americans-value-gender-equality-at-work-more-than-at-home.html
61–62 Social attitudes on same-sex marriage
www.pewforum.org/fact-sheet/changing-attitudes-on-gay-marriage

70 Bilingual children's skills
Katherine Kinzler, "The Superior Social Skills of Bilinguals," *New York Times*, 11 March 2016
www.nytimes.com/2016/03/13/opinion/sunday/the-superior-social-skills-of-bilinguals.html?_r=1

70 More positive attitudes toward native speakers
www.actfl.org/center-assessment-research-and-development/what-the-research-shows/attitudes-and-beliefs

70–71 Immerse Yourselves
Krista Byers-Heinlein and Casey Lew-Williams, "Bilingualism in the Early Years: What the Science Says," *LEARNing Landscapes* (2013) Vol. 7, no. 1.

"Bilingual children have a better 'working memory' than monolingual children," *Science Codex* (February 20, 2013). www.sciencecodex.com/bilingual_children_have_a_better_working_memory_than_monolingual_children-107222

Diane Poulin-Dubois, Agnes Blaye, Julie Coutya, Ellen Bialystok, "The effects of bilingualism on toddlers' executive functioning," *Journal of Experimental Child Psychology* (2010).

Anat Prior and Brian MacWhinney, "A bilingual advantage in task switching by in Bilingualism," *Language and Cognition* (2010) 13(02): 253.

Claudia Dreifus, "The Bilingual Advantage," *New York Times* (2013) www.nytimes.com/2011/05/31/science/31conversation.html?_r=2

BUILD A COMMUNITY

104 Child labor in Ghana and Ivory Coast
cocoainitiative.org/wp-content/uploads/2018/10/Cocoa-Report_181004_V15-FNL_digital.pdf

104 Modern slavery
www.ilo.org/global/topics/forced-labour/lang--en/index.htm

117 Social networks have tangible impact on physical health
www.kingsfund.org.uk/projects/improving-publics-health/strong-communities-wellbeing-and-resilience

PLAY TOGETHER

173 Importance of playtime
thegeniusofplay.org/genius/expert-advice/articles/playtime-is-a-back-to-school-essential.aspx#.YGd8FRNKjUI

182 Study into early childhood education
Melissa S. Kearney and Phillip B. Levine, "Early Childhood Education by MOOC: Lessons from Sesame Street," NBER Working Papers 21229, National Bureau of Economic Research, Inc. (2015). www.nber.org/system/files/working_papers/w21229/w21229.pdf

EXPLORE TOGETHER

197 260 million children out of school
www.un.org/sustainabledevelopment/education/

197 Illiterate adults
www.oxfam.org/en/press-releases/worlds-billionaires-have-more-wealth-46-billion-people

197 Husbands can legally stop their wives from working
www.un.org/sustainabledevelopment/gender-equality/

197 World poverty
www.un.org/sustainabledevelopment/poverty/

197 US child poverty
www.americanprogress.org/issues/poverty/reports/2021/01/12/494506/basic-facts-children-poverty/

198 World religions
www.weforum.org/agenda/2019/03/this-is-the-best-and-simplest-world-map-of-religions
www.pewresearch.org/fact-tank/2014/07/22/in-30-countries-heads-of-state-must-belong-to-a-certain-religion/

198 Religious violence has increased
www.weforum.org/agenda/2019/02/how-should-faith-communities-halt-the-rise-in-religious-violence/

199 1.3 billion tons of food wasted
www.un.org/press/en/2019/ga12131.doc.htm

RESOURCES

FURTHER READING

21 Books to Share

3–7 years: *The Secret of Black Rock* by Joe Todd-Stanton (Flying Eye Books)

3–8 years: *The Curious Garden* by Peter Brown (Little, Brown)

8 years and up: *The Boy who Harnessed the Wind* by William Kamkwamba and Bryan Mealer (HarperCollins)

61 Identity Matters

3–7 years: *What Happened to You?* by James Catchpole, illustrated by Karen George (Faber)

12 years and up: *Black and British: A Short, Essential History* by David Olusoga (Macmillan)

63 Princess Like Me

5–7 years: *Princess Cupcake Jones series* by Ylleya Fields, illustrated by Michael LaDuca (Belle Publishing LLC)

5–8 years: *Princess Grace series* by Mary Hoffman (Lincoln Children's Books)

5—8 years: *Princess in Black series* by Shannon Hale and Dean Hale, illustrated by LeUyen Pham (Candlewick Press)

155 Vote With Your Feet

3–7 years: *Grace for President* by Kelly DiPucchio, illustrated by LeUyen Pham (Hyperion)

5–8 years: *Vote for Our Future* by Margaret McNamara, illustrated by Micah Player (Crown)

A Vote is a Powerful Thing by Catherine Stier, illustrated by Courtney Dawson (Albert Whitman & Company)

6–9 years: *Granddaddy's Turn: A Journey to the Ballot Box* by Michael S. Bandy and Eric Stein, illustrated by James E. Ransome (Candlewick Press)

5 years and up: *The Election* by Eleanor Levenson, illustrated by Marek Jagucki (Fisherton Press)

164 Raising Curious Kids

3–7 years: *The Name Jar* by Yangsook Choi (Dragonfly Books)

8–12 years: *Little House on the Prairie* by Laura Ingalls Wilder (Egmont)

Children's TV: *Team UmiZoomie* (Nick Jr.), *My World Kitchen* (CBeebies)

167 Try It Out

All ages: *Gender Swapped Fairy Tales* by Karrie Fransman and Jonathan Plackett (Faber)

193 Carried Away

3–6 years: *Fry Bread: A Native American Family Story* by Kevin Noble Maillard, illustrated by Juana Martinez-Neal (Roaring Brook Press)

4–8 years: *Bilal Cooks Daal* by Aisha Saeed, illustrated by Anoosha Syed (Simon & Schuster)

4–8 years: *Amy Wu and the Perfect Bao* by Kat Zhang, illustrated by Charlene Chua (Simon & Schuster)

WEBSITES

Action for Nature
actionfornature.org

American Horticultural Society
ahsgardening.org

Amnesty International
amnesty.org

Autism Society
autism-society.org

BusinessGreen
businessgreen.com

Centers for Disease Control and Prevention
www.cdc.gov

Childline
childline.org

Common Sense Media
commonsensemedia.org

Council for Disabled Children
councilfordisabledchildren.org

Freecycle
freecycle.org

Malala Fund
malala.org

Motion Picture Association
motionpictures.org

Natural History Museum
nhm.org

Nextdoor
nextdoor.com

Oxfam
oxfamamerica.org

Roots & Shoots
rootsandshoots.org

Save the Children
savethechildren.org

Solidarity Sports
solidaritysports.org

The Good Shopping Guide
thegoodshoppingguide.com

Trash Nothing
trashnothing.com

Twinkl
twinkl.com

Unicef
unicef.org

World Wildlife Fund
worldwildlife.org

Youth for Human Rights
youthforhumanrights.org

Youth for Our Planet
youthforourplanet.com

INDEX

ABOUT THE AUTHOR

Anna Davidson is the author of *A Young Citizen's Guide to Money* and, as a writer and editor, specializes in books for parents and families. A mother of three, Anna read modern languages at Oxford University and spent a year teaching secondary-school English in Marseilles where she first developed a taste for global citizenship. Since then, she has worked for leading publishing houses in both London and Paris. Anna now lives and works from home in Kent. @AnnaMcDavidson

ABOUT THE ILLUSTRATOR

Cecilia Castelli is an Italian illustrator currently based in Barcelona. She creates intriguing images that aim to tell a story in a simple way, and her work has been described as bright, optimistic, and full of humanity. When Cecilia is not drawing, she's usually thinking about what she'll draw next. Insta: @BeingCecilia

AUTHOR'S ACKNOWLEDGMENTS

I'd like to thank Dawn Henderson at DK for proposing this absorbing and rewarding project, and Marianne Markham and Alastair Laing for expertly shepherding it through. Thank you also to Mandy Earey and to Annabelle, Fariba, James, Jen, Jess, Marvyn, and Melernie for making it such a pleasure to work on and for being excellent collaborators, especially throughout lockdown and homeschooling. Thanks as well to Cecilia Castelli for the fabulous illustrations. This book is dedicated to families everywhere.

PUBLISHER'S ACKNOWLEDGMENTS

Letting Go, Fair Society, Power of Speech, Stand Up for Your Beliefs, Finding Your Tribe, Political Awakening, Owning Your Identity copyright © 2021 Marvyn Harrison

On Our Bikes, Where Are You From?, Immerse Yourselves, Talking Their Language, New Ways to Celebrate, Global Playground, Travel Is an Education copyright © 2021 Dr. Annabelle Humanes

Model Citizens, Solidarity Sports, Team Goals, Reasonable Questions, Finding a Narrative, Taking Play Seriously, A Good Experience, Embracing the New copyright © 2021 Dr. Melernie Meheux

Generation Revolution, Driving Change, Sharing Stories, Informed Choices, Be True, Positive Force, Economy Ecology, The Start of History copyright © 2021 James Murray

The Universe in Books, Better Birthdays, Give and Take, Pizza Toppings, Stylish Solutions, Fashion Forward, Vote with Your Feet, Carried Away copyright © 2021 Jen Panaro

Greenhouse Experiment; Refuse, Reuse, Recycle; Garden Know-How; Unexpected Pals; Critical Experiment; Facts, Not Fear copyright © 2021 Jess Purcell

Princess Like Me, Talking About Race, Living Roots, Emotional Times, Life Lessons, Raising Curious Kids, Inspiring Encounters copyright © 2021 Fariba Soetan

Dorling Kindersley would like to thank Marie Lorimer for indexing and Anne Newman for proofreading.